Understanding Consumer Bankruptcy

Understanding Consumer Bankruptcy

A Guide for Businesses, Managers, and Creditors

Scott B. Kuperberg

Attorney at Law

BEP BUSINESS EXPERT PRESS

Understanding Consumer Bankruptcy: A Guide for Businesses, Managers, and Creditors

First published in 2016 by
Business Expert Press, LLC
222 East 46th Street, New York, NY 10017
www.businessexpertpress.com

ISBN-13: 978-1-63157-248-7 (paperback)
ISBN-13: 978-1-63157-249-4 (e-book)

Business Expert Press Business Law Collection

Collection ISSN: 2333-6722 (print)
Collection ISSN: 2333-6730 (electronic)

Cover and interior design by Exeter Premedia Services Private Ltd., Chennai, India

First edition: 2016

10 9 8 7 6 5 4 3 2 1

Printed in the United States of America.

For Ma. May your memory be a blessing...

Abstract

Any company that does business with consumers will find itself in bankruptcy court at some time during the life of the company. If you are the owner or manager of a business, you know the reality and need to understand how a customer's bankruptcy case will impact your business. Consumer bankruptcy filings have increased dramatically in the last 10 years. Businesses need to understand the bankruptcy process from the position of a creditor facing a consumer debtor. This book will provide an overview of the most common forms of consumer bankruptcy, including a timeline of events, and the creditor's interaction with the various parties along the way. We will also go through the forms every creditor will see in a bankruptcy case, and break them down so a business owner can understand what they're reading. We provide guide points for discussion with the business's attorney. Also see strategic tips and points for maximizing returns through best business practices. Several different industries are covered, including consumer lenders, vendors, community associations, and landlords.

Keywords

bankruptcy, business creditor, Chapter 7, Chapter 13, community association, consumer bankruptcy, consumer credit, consumer debt, consumer debtor, consumer finance, creditor, customer finance, debtor, homeowners association, in-house finance, landlord, lender, mortgage lender, store, supplier, tenant, vender

Contents

Disclaimers

This book is intended as a general information resource and does not constitute legal advice in any jurisdiction in the United States or anywhere in the world. Before undertaking legal action of any kind, consult with a licensed attorney in your jurisdiction. Purchase or use of this book does not create or establish an attorney–client relationship between the author, editors, publisher, or consultants, and any purchasers, readers, or viewers.

The sample documents used herein are matters of public record and are available for retrieval via the United States Federal Court System's PACER website. The documents were selected purely for illustrative purposes and are not meant to imply anything regarding the underlying cases which, to the author's knowledge, are all closed and concluded.

Some of the standard sample forms contained herein are being revised by the Administrative Office of the United States District Court. The revisions will be phased in by 2016. The information contained in the revised forms will be the same as the forms herein. Only the format of the forms will change. Please be advised that from January 2016 forward, you may see these revised forms in the course of your business.

Preface

Questions to Discuss with Your Attorney

In my years practicing bankruptcy law, I've compiled a number of things that I say to every client who sits in my conference room. I offer these suggested questions at the outset because you may meet with your attorney before familiarizing yourself with the inner workings of the bankruptcy case that you've been thrust into. These are some of the issues we will consider in this text. If you meet with your attorney after reading the book, I hope that you will revise and add to the questions to fit your particular circumstance.

Since no one reads disclaimers before the table of contents, I'll say this again: I am not your attorney. By reading this book we do not form an attorney–client relationship. While you will learn valuable information to navigate a bankruptcy case as a creditor, it is no substitute for the advice of a competent attorney, who will know your particular case and situation.

- At all times, be completely upfront and honest with your attorney. The number 1 problem attorneys have with clients is clients that withhold information, whether intentionally or unintentionally. You can never say too much to your attorney. Whatever is irrelevant, an attorney can filter out. But you never know what tidbit of information will turn your case.
- Tell your attorney about your business. We're smart, but we don't know the operational details of every business and industry. Tell your attorney how things work in your field. It's your business, you're the expert.
- Attorneys hate surprises. Give your attorney all of the information and documents that you have in your possession.
- Ask about fees. Don't be shy when it comes to money. Your attorney should be able to lay out a clear fee schedule and

provide options. For certain cases, an hourly fee is appropriate. For others, a flat fee or project-based fee is more appropriate. Be flexible and honest.

- Are you a secured or unsecured creditor? This is of primary importance to your case.
- If you believe you are a secured creditor, do you have a perfected security interest? A perfected security interest means that your lien on a loan's collateral has been filed and recorded properly in the appropriate state or county records, and has been properly signed and witnessed.
- What documents does the attorney need? Be prepared to give over everything. But find out specifically what the attorney wants to see.
- What are the chances of recovering money? After reviewing the petition, in most cases, the attorney can tell you pretty quickly where you stand.
- How will the attorney deal with a debtor who lies, obscures, and tries to mislead the court?
- Is the attorney experienced in this area? Has the attorney represented clients in your industry?
- Fraudulent Transfer—This is a big issue and could fill a book on its own. As we mention later, the bankruptcy court is very concerned about transfers and payments made by the debtor before bankruptcy. The fear is that the transfer was done for the purpose of hiding money or depriving other creditors of rightful payment. There is an entire body of law, both state and federal, concerning fraudulent transfers. If you suspect that the debtor recently spirited away money, or made a large payoff before the bankruptcy case was filed, mention that to your attorney. It's also possible that other creditors may claim that your business is the recipient of a fraudulent transfer. The attorney can go over options on how to recover the money, or if you're the recipient, to keep your money. Your attorney will discuss the fraudulent transfer issue with the trustee, and will represent you in court if necessary to protect your interests.

- Are the debtors eligible to file bankruptcy? Multiple bankruptcies, financial eligibility, and improper filing can disqualify a debtor. Make sure you and your attorney are clear on the previous filing status of the debtor and how this relates to the automatic stay.

Acknowledgments

A book is the culmination of hours, days, weeks, months, and years of work. No author does it alone. First I must express gratitude to G-d, the Creator of the Universe, for blessing and sustaining my family and I to reach this day and achieve this publication. To my wife Lily, thank you for your encouragement and support through my years of work as an attorney, and the months it took to get this book published. This never could have happened without you. Go cure the world! To my in-laws and my kids: The love and support of family has made my life during these last 10 years. To my father: I did my homework, now the Jets should win the Super Bowl. To my peer reviewers, Floyd Dickens, III, Esq. and Francesca Malenky, thank you for your unending assistance. Any errors in this book are mine and mine alone. To the publishers and staff at Business Expert Press and Momentum Press: Thank you for your hard work and patience throughout the writing process, and for the opportunity to bring this work to the public. To the hundreds of colleagues, staff, judges, and clients I've worked with over the years ... this is all your fault.

Introduction

It's the most frustrating moment for any business owner. A regular client has ordered your product on credit. Payment is late, again. You call, send letters, and get the runaround. "The check is in the mail," the customer pleads. But there is no check. Instead, you get a Notice of Bankruptcy. Filled with legalese, names, and dates, you throw up your hands in frustration. What does this mean? Will we ever get paid? Can we get our products back? How much do we have to pay a lawyer to deal with this?

When businesses encounter consumer bankruptcy, it can be a frustrating and confusing experience. Bankruptcy is a process governed by federal law, with some state law flavoring sprinkled in. The Federal Bankruptcy Code (the Code), set out in Title 11 of the United States Code, is hundreds of pages of laws and procedures that govern the five different "chapters" of bankruptcy.

CHAPTER I

What Is Bankruptcy and Why Are We Here?

Bankruptcy is a legal process that takes place within the federal court system. The purpose is to help people and businesses that are insolvent get relief from impossible-to-pay debts. Bankruptcy is meant to be a last resort. When a debtor has tried everything to make money to continue to pay debts and maintain their business or basic living standard, and failed, the debtor can turn to the bankruptcy court for protection from creditors and to unwind their financial situation.

People and entities can file for bankruptcy protection, meaning, human beings and corporate entities like corporations, limited liability companies, and every other entity that various state laws allow. We will distinguish between consumer bankruptcy, cases where the debtor is a person (with or without their small business), and business bankruptcy, cases filed by corporate entities. We will deal only with consumer bankruptcy.

The two most common types of consumer bankruptcy are Chapter 7 and Chapter 13. This refers to Title 11, Chapter 7 and Chapter 13 of the Code. It's written as 11 U.S.C. § 700, et seq., or 11 U.S.C. § 1300, et seq. on the various bankruptcy forms you'll see. Chapter 7 is personal liquidation of assets. Chapter 13 is personal reorganization. Chapter 7 also covers certain small businesses below a financial threshold that are liquidating. As a business owner, you will often see a personal Chapter 7, either just with an individual customer or coupled with the debtor's small business.

- **Bankruptcy Abuse Prevention and Consumer Protection Act of 2005 (BAPCPA)**

  The BAPCPA was an overhaul of existing bankruptcy laws. It had two purposes: (1) to give debtors additional protection from creditors, freeing them from debts that were previously nondischargeable, and (2) to all but require debtors to give up their home in the event of a bankruptcy. The BAPCPA was and remains controversial. The hope was to make a system that was fairer to both debtors and creditors. Some feel that creditors got the bulk of the benefit. The heavy standards on debtors to keep their homes were a boon to the lending industry.

- **THE MOST IMPORTANT RULE FOR CREDITORS**

  I put this at the head of the book for a reason. In my opinion, it is the first, and the most important, law every bankruptcy creditor needs to know. **Once the bankruptcy case is filed (not when you're notified, when it's actually filed) an automatic stay goes into effect. This means that the creditor can take NO ACTION to collect an outstanding debt that was incurred prior to the case being filed** (11 U.S.C. § 362(a)). "No action" includes essentially everything imaginable: no phone calls, no bills, no demand letters, no seizure, and definitely no filing a lawsuit. If a lawsuit is already pending in the state or federal court, the lawsuit is frozen in place until the bankruptcy case is resolved. Violating the automatic stay carries hefty financial penalties, sometimes tens of thousands of dollars for wanton creditors (11. U.S.C. § 362(k)). See, for example, *Hubbard v. Fleet Mortgage Co.*, 810 F.2d 779 (8th Cir. 1987), upholding a fine of over $7,000 in damages, plus attorney's fees, plus cancellation of the mortgage, in contempt action against a creditor for violation of the automatic stay. So beware.

CHAPTER II

The Cast of Characters: The Players of the Bankruptcy Drama

Now that we know the basic framework of bankruptcy law, it's time to meet the various parties involved in a bankruptcy case and understand their roles in the process.

Debtors and Creditors

Debtors and creditors are the stars of the bankruptcy show. The debtor is sometimes called the petitioner, since they file a bankruptcy petition to open the case. The debtor is the subject of the bankruptcy: the party that is either liquidating or restructuring their debts. The creditor is any party that has a claim for a debt or obligation from the debtor. The debtor may owe the creditor for a past due or current debt, or may be under an obligation pursuant to an agreement (installment contract, lease, or mortgage) to pay the creditor in the future.

Debtors and creditors can be individuals, corporations, LLCs, partnerships, or even municipalities. Creditors can also be any of these types of entities.

The Bankruptcy Trustee

Once the bankruptcy case is filed, all of the debtor's assets become the "bankruptcy estate" (11 U.S.C. § 541). The estate has a trustee to manage its affairs and make sure the debtor is complying with the bankruptcy law. Each federal court district has a bankruptcy trustee, who is hired by the federal government. In most districts, the trustee has a team of attorneys that represent the trustee's office and serve in court on the trustee's behalf. In districts with large populations, the trustee's primary role is as an administrator of the trustee's office. The trustee herself will get personally involved only in major cases.

What does the trustee do? The trustee reviews the debtor's petition and schedules (documents filed with the bankruptcy petition) to make sure they comply with the applicable bankruptcy chapter. The trustee will review the debtor's finances to see if they are eligible to file bankruptcy, and if they have made a complete disclosure of all their assets, income, and debts. Most important, the trustee ascertains what assets the debtor has available to sell and pay off debts.

The trustee does this through review of the bankruptcy petition and schedules, and by holding a meeting called the 341 Meeting of Creditors (sometimes called the 341 hearing or 341 meeting). The trustee also has to determine whether the assets are encumbered, meaning a creditor already has a financial interest or lien in the particular asset, or whether the asset is "exempt." Exempt assets are belongings that the debtor gets to keep after the bankruptcy case is over (11 U.S.C. § 522). They're not subject to sale. Exempt assets are determined by state law.

In cases of suspected bankruptcy fraud, a special attorney from the United States Trustee's Office (not the local district) may get involved. Bankruptcy fraud is a very serious crime, and the U.S. Trustee will investigate and prosecute anyone defrauding creditors or the trustee to the fullest extent of the law.

The trustee does not represent the debtor or creditors, although you may find a trustee friendly to one side or the other. They represent the U.S. government and are tasked with making sure the estate is administered according to the letter of the law.

The Bankruptcy Judge

This is someone you don't see very often. The judge holds hearings and trials when the debtor, creditor, and trustee are unable to resolve matters themselves. The community of bankruptcy attorneys is a small one, and all of the players in a particular district tend to know each other and know how to resolve disputes. The judge only steps in when something goes wrong. To give you an idea of how rare that is, in the Northern District of Georgia, Rome Division (a rural area of North Georgia), there are typically 320 cases on the court's hearing docket each week. No more than two or three require a hearing before the judge. I once met a bankruptcy attorney who, despite being in bankruptcy court every week, had not argued before a judge in 20 years!

When the judge is called upon to hear a case or motion, the judge does what all judges do: hear the evidence and legal arguments, and decide which evidence gets admitted and which does not, and ultimately renders a decision.

CHAPTER III

Bankruptcy: It's a Process

You're trying to run a business and you want the bottom line, how long will this take? What are the steps in bankruptcy and what should we do along the way? I'll give you the answer all lawyers give: it depends. The first factor is what chapter you're dealing with. Chapter 7 cases are usually much faster than Chapter 13. But Chapter 13 cases are more likely to fall apart before they even get started.

Chapter 7

A Chapter 7 bankruptcy is when the debtor is liquidating his assets to pay off debts. Whatever debts cannot be paid off are discharged and no longer have to be paid. On the short end, a Chapter 7 bankruptcy could take as little as four months. If there are assets that have to be administered, a case could take a year and a half or longer.

- **Step One—The Case Begins**
  The case begins with the debtor filing a bankruptcy petition. You, as the creditor, will receive a Notice of Bankruptcy form from the bankruptcy court advising you of the date and time of the case filing, the case number, and some of your rights as a creditor. You should also receive a copy of the bankruptcy Petition and Schedules. Schedules are lists of assets and debts of the debtor. The debtor also gets a chance to list his "exempt" assets and the legal basis for the exemption. Later, we'll go through the Petition and Schedules in detail.

- **Step Two—The 341 Meeting of Creditors**
  In a typical case, within 30 to 60 days of the filing of the petition the 341 Meeting of Creditors is scheduled. Why is it called the

341 Meeting of Creditors, or 341 Hearing? Because the meeting is required by the statute 11 U.S.C. § 341.

At the meeting, the trustee will go through the Petition and Schedules with the debtor and ask questions to confirm what's already in the papers. The debtor gets a chance to tell the trustee if anything is incorrect or needs to be added. This is not uncommon. People with dozens of credit card debts or medical debts will sometimes forget one or two during the filing process.

Creditors are allowed to be present and are entitled to ask questions. A creditor may want to know the location or disposition of certain property, or whether certain property is insured. If the creditor spots an inconsistency between their records and the bankruptcy papers, the creditor may explore that as well.

In most cases, the 341 Hearing is concluded on the spot after a few minutes of questioning. Sometimes it's kept open and another meeting is scheduled for in a month to allow the debtor to present tax returns, amend his Schedules, or present additional documentation.

- **Step Three—Disposing of Assets**
  Here is where the timing of the case turns. If there are no non-exempt assets to sell or dispose of, the trustee will recommend the case be discharged. The case will likely end there within the four-month timeline. But if there are assets, what happens next depends on liens.

  In most cases, real property (houses, land, buildings) is encumbered by a mortgage. Typically, the debtor is in arrears on their mortgage. The mortgage lender will usually want the property back. But, there is an "automatic stay" in effect (see Chapter I herein). Outside of bankruptcy, the mortgage lender would be able to retake the property through a state procedure of foreclosure. Permission to retake the property during bankruptcy must be obtained from the bankruptcy court (11 § U.S.C. 362(d)). The mortgage lender will file a "motion for relief from stay" to proceed with foreclosure. In most cases, the motion for relief is unopposed by the debtor. This hearing is held within a month of the motion being filed with a consent agreement memorializing the debtor's lack of opposition to the property being foreclosed.

Occasionally, the debtor fights a motion for relief. There are numerous arguments a debtor can raise. The debtor may claim that the creditor's security interest is not perfected, meaning there is a defect in the lien documents. There can be a question of the creditor's valuation of the property. In rare cases, the debtor argues that the creditor is guilty of fraud. In these instances, the court will schedule a full hearing another month after the initial hearing.

Sometimes the debtor will have other property that is nonexempt (meaning, the debtor cannot keep it after the bankruptcy). This can include cars, boats, planes, art, jewelry, anything movable, and even real estate that is not encumbered by a lien or mortgage (meaning, all of the debts owed on it have been paid off). The nonexempt property will have to be liquidated and distributed to pay off creditors. This is when a four-month case becomes a two-year marathon.

The trustee will first gather and valuate all of the nonexempt assets of the debtor. Next, the trustee will look for buyers to obtain the highest price. This can be done through an auction, direct advertisement and sale, or through a professional broker. In whatever manner the assets are sold, the seller and the trustee take a commission. Selling assets can be quick and easy for sought-after items, or difficult for specialized property. Inevitably, there will be disputes among the trustee, debtor, and creditors over the value of the assets. Those disputes get settled by the judge.

Once the assets are sold, the proceeds get distributed to creditors in order of their priority. Priority is determined by law. Secured creditors get first crack at the proceeds. Naturally, creditors will fight over who has priority. In large cases, significant sums of money are at stake. Good attorneys will usually be able to negotiate an agreement with the trustee and other creditors setting out a fair distribution of the sale proceeds. But if an agreement cannot be reached, hearings have to be held in front of the judge.

To get a sense of how numerous hearings slow down the progress of a case, estimate a month for each hearing. This is the lead time required for a hearing to be set.

- **Step 4—Discharge**

  Once all of the assets have been disposed of, the case will be submitted to the judge to sign an order of discharge closing the case and wiping out the unpaid debts of the debtor. After disposal of assets, this can take anywhere from a few weeks to two months, depending on your district. It is an understatement to say that the courts are backlogged.

Chapter 13

Cases filed under Chapter 13 of the Bankruptcy Code follow a different timeline. In a Chapter 13 case the debtor is restructuring his debt to pay it off over time. The debtor files a "Chapter 13 Plan" along with their Schedules and Petition. The Plan shows how the debtor will repay existing past-due debt (arrearage) within a period of three to five years. The Plan also has to show that the debtor has the ability to pay recurring debts (mortgages, leases, other payment plans) and still be able to meet regular living expenses. The debtor can abandon property as part of the Plan and not have to pay debt owed toward that property. After the Plan has been completed, the debtor's unsecured debts are discharged, and the debtor is considered current on all secured debts that have been paid under the Plan.

- **Steps 1 and 2—Filing and 341 Hearing**

  Similar to Chapter 7, the trustee holds a 341 Meeting of Creditors approximately 30 days after filing of the Petition and Schedules. Unlike Chapter 7, the trustee will scrutinize the debtor's Chapter 13 Plan to make sure it's feasible. If it's not, the trustee will direct the debtor to revise his Plan, if possible, and resubmit it before going to the next step—confirmation.

- **Step 3—Confirmation**

  The Chapter 13 Plan has to be confirmed (approved) by the bankruptcy court. In most cases, the trustee and creditors have objections to the Plan in its initial form. These objections can be related to feasibility of the Plan, unfair treatment of creditors, or questionable disclosures about assets, debt, and property values. The Plan may have to go through several amendments and versions before it's confirmed.

The process of getting from filing to confirmation can average six to eight months in a typical case. If the debtor falls behind on payments during the confirmation stage, it's possible that the case could be dismissed then and there. Statistically, between 66 percent and 90 percent of Chapter 13 bankruptcy cases fail, depending on the year, and most debtors never make it to the end of their Plan (http://govinfo.library.unt.edu/nbrc/report/08consum.html).

- **Step 4—Term of the Plan and Discharge**
The bankruptcy code allows for a Plan to last from three to five years (or 36 to 60 months, as they say in the Plan). During this time, abandoned assets will be repossessed by creditors, and the debtor will make two ongoing payments to each creditor: (1) regular installment payments on mortgages and other loans, and (2) payments on arrearages owed to creditors. The arrearage payment is calculated as the amount of arrearage divided by the number of months of the Plan, plus a reduced interest rate. The arrearage amount is the amount of the back payments owed from the date of filing the bankruptcy.

If the debtor successfully makes all of these payments during the term of the Plan, then the debtor is discharged at the end, and is no longer liable for any other unpaid debts not covered by the Plan. If the debtor misses a payment, the creditors and trustee can ask for the case to be dismissed. Often, the debtor is given a few chances to catch up. If the debtor is unable to catch up or to get the creditors to agree to an amendment of the Plan, the case will be dismissed and all of the debts owed by the debtor will be restored (less payments made during the bankruptcy).

CHAPTER IV

Creditors and Their Attorneys, Is This Really Necessary?

As an attorney, I'm required by my profession to answer with an emphatic "yes." Bankruptcy is a very complicated area of the law with many forms and technicalities. But as a business owner, you have to weigh the cost of hiring an attorney against the likelihood that the attorney will be able to help you get any money out of the case. You may end up throwing good money after bad.

If the debtor is in a Chapter 7 case, and is claiming no assets, and you are not a secured creditor, there's very little an attorney can do to help you.

However, if there are assets, or you suspect the debtor is being less-than-truthful in his disclosures, you should consider hiring an attorney to push the trustee to investigate further. In other words, if there are assets, or you are a secured creditor, absolutely hire an attorney to protect your interests and the interests of the secured property. An attorney can file a motion for relief from stay that will get you out of the bankruptcy case faster than waiting until discharge. An attorney can also represent you in dealing with the trustee to maximize your portion of the sale of assets.

In the Chapter 13 context, the calculus is similar. If your business is not a secured creditor, it is unlikely that you will realize any payment from the Plan. Check the Plan anyway with an attorney. With an attorney experienced in analyzing bankruptcy cases, you will see if unsecured creditors are truly left without recourse. If you are a secured creditor, it pays to have an attorney work with you to file the Proof of Claim. In many courts, a corporate entity can file their own Proof of Claim with the bankruptcy court. However, some courts require an attorney to file on behalf of the corporation.

Bottom line: It is best to consult with an attorney regardless of the circumstances. A good attorney will tell you when their services aren't needed.

CHAPTER V

Your Rights and Duties as a Creditor

We've given you an overview of the peoples and processes involved in a bankruptcy case. Let's look more specifically at the rights and obligations your company will have as a creditor in a consumer bankruptcy case.

The Automatic Stay

The Bankruptcy Code states that once a bankruptcy case is filed, certain rights and restrictions immediately kick in. The most important restriction for both the debtor and the creditor is the automatic stay. The instant a bankruptcy case is filed, a bankruptcy estate is created and the debtor falls under the protection of the Bankruptcy Code. Protection means that all actions to collect the debt must stop immediately. Creditors cannot send letters to a debtor, make phone calls, file or continue a lawsuit, or take any steps to collect a debt that exists at the time the bankruptcy petition is filed.

While the automatic stay protects debtors from collection of existing debts, new debts are fair game. Creditors are generally allowed to take action to collect newly accrued debts. But what does this include?

An Existing Mortgage or Car Payment?

Since the entire debt owed is outstanding at the time of the bankruptcy filing, a creditor is not allowed to send demand for subsequent payments. In most mortgage and car note agreements, insolvency (bankruptcy) accelerates the debt, making the entire debt due immediately. If the creditor wishes to continue to allow the debtor to make payments and hold on to the collateral (the car or house) then the parties can enter into a Reaffirmation Agreement (discussed later).

The creditor is allowed to send a reminder note to the debtor advising of the installment payment amount due, but cannot ask for payment. This is tricky so it is best to avoid at all costs. Your attorney will communicate with the debtor's attorney about unpaid installments.

Payment on New, Post-Filing Debt

In some limited circumstances, a bankruptcy debtor can get credit or a loan after he's filed for bankruptcy protection. There are also some types of recurring debts that are not installment payments, such as homeowners association dues or condominium assessments. These types of debts generally can be collected during bankruptcy and demand is technically permissible.

HOWEVER, any attempt to collect a debt during bankruptcy is legally precarious. Keep in mind that the debtor's assets and cash are now part of an estate that is under the care of the trustee. It is best to work with your attorney to obtain relief from the automatic stay before proceeding with any type of collection activity.

Lawsuits That Are Already Pending

Any lawsuit that was pending at the time the bankruptcy case was filed is "stayed." This means the case is frozen where it is, and litigation cannot continue. It is incumbent upon both parties to notify the trial court that bankruptcy has been filed, so the court can stay the case on their docket. Actions that happen in the trial court during bankruptcy are generally void.

Co-Debtors

A co-debtor is a person obligated to pay a debt along with the bankruptcy debtor, but who is not a party to the bankruptcy case. In Chapter 7, the co-debtor does not receive any protection. But in Chapter 13, there is a co-debtor stay (11 U.S.C. § 1301). This means that a creditor cannot take any action to collect a debt against a co-debtor while the bankruptcy case is pending. To continue collecting against a co-debtor in Chapter 13, the creditor must obtain an order from the court lifting the automatic stay.

Determining Your Status as a Secured or an Unsecured Creditor

Whether you are a secured or an unsecured creditor will make or break your chances of recovering an unpaid debt in a bankruptcy case. But how do you know if you are secured or unsecured?

A secured creditor is one who has a lien on an asset of the debtor. This could mean a mortgage on real property, a lien on a car securing a car note, a UCC-1 lien on inventory and equipment, or any right to property owned by the debtor that was acquired to secure a debt. To make the creditor "secured," some sort of notice of the security must be filed with an official body. Typically this is a mortgage deed, deed of trust, or security deed filed with the county real estate clerk's office, a UCC-1 statement with the secretary of state, or a car lien filed with the department of motor vehicles. If there is no recorded, public document giving notice of the lien, then the debt and the creditor are unsecured.

An unsecured creditor is the opposite of a secured creditor. The debt owed is not secured by any property or collateral. The debtor simply promised to pay and the obligation is a matter of contract.

Chapter 7

In a Chapter 7 case, an unsecured creditor has almost no role. Most Chapter 7 cases have no assets to dispose of, so the unsecured creditor is left without recourse. The unpaid debt will be discharged with nothing paid out to the creditor. In the unlikely event that there are unencumbered, nonexempt assets in a Chapter 7 case, an unsecured creditor will be far down on the list of priorities to get paid. The secured creditors will all have to be paid off first, in full. If any money remains, unsecured creditors may get a share.

Secured creditors, however, have the right to ask the bankruptcy court to allow the creditor to seize the collateral. This is usually done with a motion for relief from stay, which will allow the creditor to use state law remedies (like foreclosure) to take the collateral. While the market value of the collateral will often be less than the debt owed, the secured creditor is not left completely empty-handed. In the rare event that the collateral is sold for more than the debt, the excess proceeds have to be returned to the trustee for distribution to other creditors. Creditors generally cannot profit in bankruptcy.

Chapter 13

In a Chapter 13 case, unsecured creditors are almost never part of the Plan. Unsecured debt gets discharged if the Plan is completed. However, if the case is dismissed either before or after confirmation of the Plan, the unsecured debts are restored. It makes sense, therefore, to monitor Chapter 13 cases to their conclusion even if you are an unsecured creditor.

Secured creditors have to be accounted for in the Plan. If an arrearage is owed, it has to be paid off as part of the Plan. The debtor also has to show how he will make installment payments based on his income. The debtor can also abandon secured property to the creditor, opening the door for foreclosure or another state law remedy of seizure.

Section 341 Hearing

At the 341 Hearing (the Meeting of Creditors), all creditors are allowed to appear and observe the meeting. Creditors are allowed to ask questions of the debtor related to their financial disclosures, intent, and condition and location of any secured property. This is also a good chance to discuss seizure of abandoned property with the debtor's attorney. Creditors rarely appear for 341 Hearings unless they suspect fraud or deception.

CHAPTER VI

Petitions, Schedules, and Forms: Understanding the Many Documents of a Bankruptcy Case

Petition and Schedules

The Petition and Schedules can range in length between 12 and 65 pages. Shorter Petitions with empty Schedules are commonly called "skeleton" petitions. They're bare bones. Skeleton Petitions are usually filed when a debtor is in a rush to file because of an immediate deadline, or in rare cases of abuse where the debtor does not intend to follow through with the bankruptcy, but merely interfere with creditors. These must be amended and completed within a certain deadline set by the bankruptcy court or the case will be dismissed.

We'll look at a Petition and Schedules used by a small family business. The business was a "sole proprietorship," not a corporation. In this case, the family owned real estate that they rented out for income. We'll go page-by-page to dissect the documents so you understand what you're looking at when you receive a Notice of Bankruptcy, and when you get a hold of the underlying documents, you'll be able to spot errors relating to your status as a creditor, and you'll be better able to discuss the case with your attorney.

Case 1:13-bk-11002   Doc 1   Filed 02/28/13   Entered 02/28/13 13:08:55   Desc Main
Document   Page 1 of 43

B1 (Official Form 1)(12/11)

United States Bankruptcy Court Eastern District of Tennessee	Voluntary Petition

Name of Debtor (if individual, enter Last, First, Middle): White, Sherrill Edward	Name of Joint Debtor (Spouse) (Last, First, Middle): White, Shirley A.
All Other Names used by the Debtor in the last 8 years (include married, maiden, and trade names): FDBA SEW Construction; FDBA Savannah Springs LLC Apartments; DBA Savannah Way LLC	All Other Names used by the Joint Debtor in the last 8 years (include married, maiden, and trade names):
Last four digits of Soc. Sec. or Individual-Taxpayer I.D. (ITIN) No./Complete EIN (if more than one, state all) xxx-xx-0357	Last four digits of Soc. Sec. or Individual-Taxpayer I.D. (ITIN) No./Complete EIN (if more than one, state all) xxx-xx-1224
Street Address of Debtor (No. and Street, City, and State): 2989 Salem Valley Road Ringgold, GA ZIP Code 30736	Street Address of Joint Debtor (No. and Street, City, and State): 2989 Salem Valley Road Ringgold, GA ZIP Code 30736
County of Residence or of the Principal Place of Business: Catoosa	County of Residence or of the Principal Place of Business: Catoosa
Mailing Address of Debtor (if different from street address): PO Box 9905 Chattanooga, TN ZIP Code 37412	Mailing Address of Joint Debtor (if different from street address): PO Box 9905 Chattanooga, TN ZIP Code 37412
Location of Principal Assets of Business Debtor (if different from street address above):	

Type of Debtor (Form of Organization) (Check one box)
- ☑ Individual (includes Joint Debtors) *See Exhibit D on page 2 of this form.*
- ☐ Corporation (includes LLC and LLP)
- ☐ Partnership
- ☐ Other (If debtor is not one of the above entities, check this box and state type of entity below.)

Chapter 15 Debtors
Country of debtor's center of main interests:

Each country in which a foreign proceeding by, regarding, or against debtor is pending:

Nature of Business (Check one box)
- ☐ Health Care Business
- ☐ Single Asset Real Estate as defined in 11 U.S.C. § 101 (51B)
- ☐ Railroad
- ☐ Stockbroker
- ☐ Commodity Broker
- ☐ Clearing Bank
- ☐ Other

Tax-Exempt Entity (Check box, if applicable)
- ☐ Debtor is a tax-exempt organization under Title 26 of the United States Code (the Internal Revenue Code).

Chapter of Bankruptcy Code Under Which the Petition is Filed (Check one box)
- ☐ Chapter 7
- ☐ Chapter 9
- ☐ Chapter 11
- ☐ Chapter 12
- ☑ Chapter 13
- ☐ Chapter 15 Petition for Recognition of a Foreign Main Proceeding
- ☐ Chapter 15 Petition for Recognition of a Foreign Nonmain Proceeding

Nature of Debts (Check one box)
- ☑ Debts are primarily consumer debts, defined in 11 U.S.C. § 101(8) as "incurred by an individual primarily for a personal, family, or household purpose."
- ☐ Debts are primarily business debts.

Filing Fee (Check one box)
- ☐ Full Filing Fee attached
- ☑ Filing Fee to be paid in installments (applicable to individuals only). Must attach signed application for the court's consideration certifying that the debtor is unable to pay fee except in installments. Rule 1006(b). See Official Form 3A.
- ☐ Filing Fee waiver requested (applicable to chapter 7 individuals only). Must attach signed application for the court's consideration. See Official Form 3B.

Chapter 11 Debtors
Check one box:
- ☐ Debtor is a small business debtor as defined in 11 U.S.C. § 101(51D).
- ☐ Debtor is not a small business debtor as defined in 11 U.S.C. § 101(51D).

Check if:
- ☐ Debtor's aggregate noncontingent liquidated debts (excluding debts owed to insiders or affiliates) are less than $2,343,300 (amount subject to adjustment on 4/01/13 and every three years thereafter).

Check all applicable boxes:
- ☐ A plan is being filed with this petition.
- ☐ Acceptances of the plan were solicited prepetition from one or more classes of creditors, in accordance with 11 U.S.C. § 1126(b).

Statistical/Administrative Information
- ☑ Debtor estimates that funds will be available for distribution to unsecured creditors.
- ☐ Debtor estimates that, after any exempt property is excluded and administrative expenses paid, there will be no funds available for distribution to unsecured creditors.

THIS SPACE IS FOR COURT USE ONLY

Estimated Number of Creditors

☑	☐	☐	☐	☐	☐	☐	☐	☐	☐
1-49	50-99	100-199	200-999	1,000-5,000	5,001-10,000	10,001-25,000	25,001-50,000	50,001-100,000	OVER 100,000

Estimated Assets

☐	☐	☐	☑	☐	☐	☐	☐	☐	☐
$0 to $50,000	$50,001 to $100,000	$100,001 to $500,000	$500,001 to $1 million	$1,000,001 to $10 million	$10,000,001 to $50 million	$50,000,001 to $100 million	$100,000,001 to $500 million	$500,000,001 to $1 billion	More than $1 billion

Estimated Liabilities

☐	☐	☐	☐	☑	☐	☐	☐	☐	☐
$0 to $50,000	$50,001 to $100,000	$100,001 to $500,000	$500,001 to $1 million	$1,000,001 to $10 million	$10,000,001 to $50 million	$50,000,001 to $100 million	$100,000,001 to $500 million	$500,000,001 to $1 billion	More than $1 billion

- Here the debtor (or debtors) gives their personal information and the names of any related businesses. Check the list of names against your information for the debtor to see if they left out any business names.
- The debtor also states the chapter of bankruptcy, and whether they're filing as an individual or a corporate entity.
- Whether the debtor believes funds will be available to distribute to unsecured creditors is also stated on this page. This is a flag for unsecured creditors to take notice of a case.

Case 1:13-bk-11002   Doc 1   Filed 02/28/13   Entered 02/28/13 13:08:55   Desc Main
Document   Page 2 of 43

B1 (Official Form 1)(12/11)

Voluntary Petition	Name of Debtor(s):
(This page must be completed and filed in every case)	**White, Sherrill Edward** **White, Shirley A.**

All Prior Bankruptcy Cases Filed Within Last 8 Years (If more than two, attach additional sheet)		
Location Where Filed: **- None -**	Case Number:	Date Filed:
Location Where Filed:	Case Number:	Date Filed:

Pending Bankruptcy Case Filed by any Spouse, Partner, or Affiliate of this Debtor (If more than one, attach additional sheet)		
Name of Debtor: - None -	Case Number:	Date Filed:
District:	Relationship:	Judge:

Exhibit A	Exhibit B
	(To be completed if debtor is an individual whose debts are primarily consumer debts.)
(To be completed if debtor is required to file periodic reports (e.g., forms 10K and 10Q) with the Securities and Exchange Commission pursuant to Section 13 or 15(d) of the Securities Exchange Act of 1934 and is requesting relief under chapter 11.)	I, the attorney for the petitioner named in the foregoing petition, declare that I have informed the petitioner that [he or she] may proceed under chapter 7, 11, 12, or 13 of title 11, United States Code, and have explained the relief available under each such chapter. I further certify that I delivered to the debtor the notice required by 11 U.S.C. §342(b).

☐ Exhibit A is attached and made a part of this petition.	X */s/ Brent James* __February 28, 2013__
	     Signature of Attorney for Debtor(s) (Date)
	     Brent James TN18308/GA388855

Exhibit C

Does the debtor own or have possession of any property that poses or is alleged to pose a threat of imminent and identifiable harm to public health or safety?

☐ Yes, and Exhibit C is attached and made a part of this petition.

■ No.

Exhibit D

(To be completed by every individual debtor. If a joint petition is filed, each spouse must complete and attach a separate Exhibit D.)

■ Exhibit D completed and signed by the debtor is attached and made a part of this petition.

If this is a joint petition:

■ Exhibit D also completed and signed by the joint debtor is attached and made a part of this petition.

Information Regarding the Debtor - Venue
(Check any applicable box)

☐ Debtor has been domiciled or has had a residence, principal place of business, or principal assets in this District for 180 days immediately preceding the date of this petition or for a longer part of such 180 days than in any other District.

☐ There is a bankruptcy case concerning debtor's affiliate, general partner, or partnership pending in this District.

☐ Debtor is a debtor in a foreign proceeding and has its principal place of business or principal assets in the United States in this District, or has no principal place of business or assets in the United States but is a defendant in an action or proceeding [in a federal or state court] in this District, or the interests of the parties will be served in regard to the relief sought in this District.

Certification by a Debtor Who Resides as a Tenant of Residential Property
(Check all applicable boxes)

☐ Landlord has a judgment against the debtor for possession of debtor's residence. (If box checked, complete the following.)

_____
(Name of landlord that obtained judgment)

_____
(Address of landlord)

☐ Debtor claims that under applicable nonbankruptcy law, there are circumstances under which the debtor would be permitted to cure the entire monetary default that gave rise to the judgment for possession, after the judgment for possession was entered, and

☐ Debtor has included in this petition the deposit with the court of any rent that would become due during the 30-day period after the filing of the petition.

☐ Debtor certifies that he/she has served the Landlord with this certification. (11 U.S.C. § 362(l)).

- On this page, the debtor lists all of his prior bankruptcy cases. This is important because of the automatic stay. If a debtor has filed more than one case within 180 days (e.g., if the first one was dismissed), then the stay may only last for 30 days. More cases within 365 days or two years bring about a presumption of abuse. Carefully discuss this section with your attorney. This will be implications for how the case will proceed.

B1 (Official Form 1)(12/11)   Page 3

| Voluntary Petition | Name of Debtor(s): |
| *(This page must be completed and filed in every case)* | White, Sherrill Edward
White, Shirley A. |

Signatures

Signature(s) of Debtor(s) (Individual/Joint)	Signature of a Foreign Representative
I declare under penalty of perjury that the information provided in this petition is true and correct. [If petitioner is an individual whose debts are primarily consumer debts and has chosen to file under chapter 7] I am aware that I may proceed under chapter 7, 11, 12, or 13 of title 11, United States Code, understand the relief available under each such chapter, and choose to proceed under chapter 7. [If no attorney represents me and no bankruptcy petition preparer signs the petition] I have obtained and read the notice required by 11 U.S.C. §342(b). I request relief in accordance with the chapter of title 11, United States Code, specified in this petition.	I declare under penalty of perjury that the information provided in this petition is true and correct, that I am the foreign representative of a debtor in a foreign proceeding, and that I am authorized to file this petition. (Check only one box.) ☐ I request relief in accordance with chapter 15 of title 11. United States Code. Certified copies of the documents required by 11 U.S.C. §1515 are attached. ☐ Pursuant to 11 U.S.C. §1511, I request relief in accordance with the chapter of title 11 specified in this petition. A certified copy of the order granting recognition of the foreign main proceeding is attached.

X /s/ **Sherrill Edward White**
   Signature of Debtor Sherrill Edward White
	X _____
	   Signature of Foreign Representative

X /s/ **Shirley A. White** Signature of Joint Debtor Shirley A. White	Printed Name of Foreign Representative
	Date
Telephone Number (If not represented by attorney)	**Signature of Non-Attorney Bankruptcy Petition Preparer**
February 28, 2013 Date	I declare under penalty of perjury that: (1) I am a bankruptcy petition preparer as defined in 11 U.S.C. § 110; (2) I prepared this document for compensation and have provided the debtor with a copy of this document and the notices and information required under 11 U.S.C. §§ 110(b), 110(h), and 342(b); and, (3) if rules or guidelines have been promulgated pursuant to 11 U.S.C. § 110(h) setting a maximum fee for services chargeable by bankruptcy petition preparers, I have given the debtor notice of the maximum amount before preparing any document for filing for a debtor or accepting any fee from the debtor, as required in that section. Official Form 19 is attached.
Signature of Attorney*	
X /s/ **Brent James** Signature of Attorney for Debtor(s)	
Brent James TN18308/GA388855 Printed Name of Attorney for Debtor(s)	Printed Name and title, if any, of Bankruptcy Petition Preparer
Harriss & Hartman Law Firm, P. C. Firm Name	

P. O. Drawer 220
  200 McFarland Building
  Rossville, GA 30741
   Address
	Social-Security number (If the bankruptcy petition preparer is not an individual, state the Social Security number of the officer, principal, responsible person or partner of the bankruptcy petition preparer.)(Required by 11 U.S.C. § 110.)

Email: BKCourts@HarrissHartman.com
  (706) 861-0203 Fax: (706) 861-6838
   Telephone Number	

February 28, 2013 Date	Address
*In a case in which § 707(b)(4)(D) applies, this signature also constitutes a certification that the attorney has no knowledge after an inquiry that the information in the schedules is incorrect.	X _____
	Date
Signature of Debtor (Corporation/Partnership)	Signature of bankruptcy petition preparer or officer, principal, responsible person, or partner whose Social Security number is provided above.
I declare under penalty of perjury that the information provided in this petition is true and correct, and that I have been authorized to file this petition on behalf of the debtor. The debtor requests relief in accordance with the chapter of title 11, United States Code, specified in this petition.	Names and Social-Security numbers of all other individuals who prepared or assisted in preparing this document unless the bankruptcy petition preparer is not an individual:
X _____ Signature of Authorized Individual	
Printed Name of Authorized Individual	If more than one person prepared this document, attach additional sheets conforming to the appropriate official form for each person.
Title of Authorized Individual	*A bankruptcy petition preparer's failure to comply with the provisions of title 11 and the Federal Rules of Bankruptcy Procedure may result in fines or imprisonment or both. 11 U.S.C. §110; 18 U.S.C. §156.*
Date	

- While this is simply a signature page, it is very important. The debtor is affirming under penalty of perjury that everything contained in the Petition and Schedules is correct. The debtor risks massive fines and years in jail for lying on these forms. It is not uncommon for creditors' attorneys to wave this page in front of debtors of questionable character.

Case 1:13-bk-11002   Doc 1   Filed 02/28/13   Entered 02/28/13 13:08:55   Desc Main
Document   Page 4 of 43

B 1D (Official Form 1, Exhibit D) (12/09)

United States Bankruptcy Court
Eastern District of Tennessee

In re   **Sherrill Edward White**
        Shirley A. White _____   Case No. _____
                                        Debtor(s)   Chapter   13

EXHIBIT D - INDIVIDUAL DEBTOR'S STATEMENT OF COMPLIANCE WITH CREDIT COUNSELING REQUIREMENT

Warning: You must be able to check truthfully one of the five statements regarding credit counseling listed below. If you cannot do so, you are not eligible to file a bankruptcy case, and the court can dismiss any case you do file. If that happens, you will lose whatever filing fee you paid, and your creditors will be able to resume collection activities against you. If your case is dismissed and you file another bankruptcy case later, you may be required to pay a second filing fee and you may have to take extra steps to stop creditors' collection activities.

Every individual debtor must file this Exhibit D. If a joint petition is filed, each spouse must complete and file a separate Exhibit D. Check one of the five statements below and attach any documents as directed.

■ 1. Within the 180 days before the filing of my bankruptcy case, I received a briefing from a credit counseling agency approved by the United States trustee or bankruptcy administrator that outlined the opportunities for available credit counseling and assisted me in performing a related budget analysis, and I have a certificate from the agency describing the services provided to me. *Attach a copy of the certificate and a copy of any debt repayment plan developed through the agency.*

□ 2. Within the 180 days before the filing of my bankruptcy case, I received a briefing from a credit counseling agency approved by the United States trustee or bankruptcy administrator that outlined the opportunities for available credit counseling and assisted me in performing a related budget analysis, but I do not have a certificate from the agency describing the services provided to me. *You must file a copy of a certificate from the agency describing the services provided to you and a copy of any debt repayment plan developed through the agency no later than 14 days after your bankruptcy case is filed.*

□ 3. I certify that I requested credit counseling services from an approved agency but was unable to obtain the services during the seven days from the time I made my request, and the following exigent circumstances merit a temporary waiver of the credit counseling requirement so I can file my bankruptcy case now. *[Summarize exigent circumstances here.]* ___

If your certification is satisfactory to the court, you must still obtain the credit counseling briefing within the first 30 days after you file your bankruptcy petition and promptly file a certificate from the agency that provided the counseling, together with a copy of any debt management plan developed through the agency. Failure to fulfill these requirements may result in dismissal of your case. Any extension of the 30-day deadline can be granted only for cause and is limited to a maximum of 15 days. Your case may also be dismissed if the court is not satisfied with your reasons for filing your bankruptcy case without first receiving a credit counseling briefing.

Software Copyright (c) 1996-2013 CCH INCORPORATED - www.bestcase.com   Best Case Bankruptcy

- The Bankruptcy Code requires all debtors to undergo two financial management seminars. One must be taken before the bankruptcy case is filed and one must be taken within a number of days after filing. The debtor must certify that he completed, or will complete, these courses and file the certificates of completion.

B 1D (Official Form 1, Exhibit D) (12/09) - Cont.   Page 2

☐ 4. I am not required to receive a credit counseling briefing because of: *[Check the applicable statement.]* *[Must be accompanied by a motion for determination by the court.]*
☐ Incapacity. (Defined in 11 U.S.C. § 109(h)(4) as impaired by reason of mental illness or mental deficiency so as to be incapable of realizing and making rational decisions with respect to financial responsibilities.);
☐ Disability. (Defined in 11 U.S.C. § 109(h)(4) as physically impaired to the extent of being unable, after reasonable effort, to participate in a credit counseling briefing in person, by telephone, or through the Internet.);
☐ Active military duty in a military combat zone.

☐ 5. The United States trustee or bankruptcy administrator has determined that the credit counseling requirement of 11 U.S.C. § 109(h) does not apply in this district.

I certify under penalty of perjury that the information provided above is true and correct.

Signature of Debtor: /s/ Sherrill Edward White
                        Sherrill Edward White

Date: February 28, 2013

- The financial management and counseling course is fairly standardized and can be taken online from a number of providers. It is inexpensive, ranging from $25 to $50 per course. I personally recommend that everyone take a financial management or counseling seminar to better manage their personal finances.

B7 (Official Form 7) (12/12)

United States Bankruptcy Court
Eastern District of Tennessee

In re   Sherrill Edward White
        Shirley A. White   Case No. _____
                              Debtor(s)   Chapter   13

STATEMENT OF FINANCIAL AFFAIRS

This statement is to be completed by every debtor. Spouses filing a joint petition may file a single statement on which the information for both spouses is combined. If the case is filed under chapter 12 or chapter 13, a married debtor must furnish information for both spouses whether or not a joint petition is filed, unless the spouses are separated and a joint petition is not filed. An individual debtor engaged in business as a sole proprietor, partner, family farmer, or self-employed professional, should provide the information requested on this statement concerning all such activities as well as the individual's personal affairs. To indicate payments, transfers and the like to minor children, state the child's initials and the name and address of the child's parent or guardian, such as "A.B., a minor child, by John Doe, guardian." Do not disclose the child's name. See, 11 U.S.C. § 112; Fed. R. Bankr. P. 1007(m).

Questions 1 - 18 are to be completed by all debtors. Debtors that are or have been in business, as defined below, also must complete Questions 19 - 25. If the answer to an applicable question is "None," mark the box labeled "None." If additional space is needed for the answer to any question, use and attach a separate sheet properly identified with the case name, case number (if known), and the number of the question.

DEFINITIONS

"In business." A debtor is "in business" for the purpose of this form if the debtor is a corporation or partnership. An individual debtor is "in business" for the purpose of this form if the debtor is or has been, within six years immediately preceding the filing of this bankruptcy case, any of the following: an officer, director, managing executive, or owner of 5 percent or more of the voting or equity securities of a corporation; a partner, other than a limited partner, of a partnership; a sole proprietor or self-employed full-time or part-time. An individual debtor also may be "in business" for the purpose of this form if the debtor engages in a trade, business, or other activity, other than as an employee, to supplement income from the debtor's primary employment.

"Insider." The term "insider" includes but is not limited to: relatives of the debtor; general partners of the debtor and their relatives; corporations of which the debtor is an officer, director, or person in control; officers, directors, and any persons in control of a corporate debtor and their relatives; affiliates of the debtor and insiders of such affiliates; and any managing agent of the debtor. 11 U.S.C. § 101(2), (31).

---

1. Income from employment or operation of business

None ☐

State the gross amount of income the debtor has received from employment, trade, or profession, or from operation of the debtor's business, including part-time activities either as an employee or in independent trade or business, from the beginning of this calendar year to the date this case was commenced. State also the gross amounts received during the two years immediately preceding this calendar year. (A debtor that maintains, or has maintained, financial records on the basis of a fiscal rather than a calendar year may report fiscal year income. Identify the beginning and ending dates of the debtor's fiscal year.) If a joint petition is filed, state income for each spouse separately. (Married debtors filing under chapter 12 or chapter 13 must state income of both spouses whether or not a joint petition is filed, unless the spouses are separated and a joint petition is not filed.)

AMOUNT	SOURCE
$-215,992.00	Joint Income for 2012

---

2. Income other than from employment or operation of business

None ☐

State the amount of income received by the debtor other than from employment, trade, profession, or operation of the debtor's business during the two years immediately preceding the commencement of this case. Give particulars. If a joint petition is filed, state income for each spouse separately. (Married debtors filing under chapter 12 or chapter 13 must state income for each spouse whether or not a joint petition is filed, unless the spouses are separated and a joint petition is not filed.)

AMOUNT	SOURCE
$1,482.00	Debtor receives monthly social security
$875.00	Debtor receives interest payment monthly for five years on the Savannah Springs Apartments (93 units)

- Here begins the Statement of Financial Affairs. The debtor must disclose all income for the three years preceding bankruptcy.
- Section 1 requires disclosure of all income from employment. A negative number in this section is odd (since either you make more or you don't from employment, but you can't lose money). In this case, the debtors were examined by the trustee in detail about their income.
- Section 2 requires disclosure of all income from business operations and the source.

Case 1:13-bk-11002   Doc 1   Filed 02/28/13   Entered 02/28/13 13:08:55   Desc Main
Document   Page 9 of 43

B 7 (12/12)   2

AMOUNT	SOURCE
$750.00	Joint Debtor receives monthly social security
$305.66	Debtor receives monthly second mortgage payments from Valerie & Stephen Fraley for 2509 Saint Lucie Court, Chattanooga TN 37421

3. Payments to creditors

None ☐ *Complete a. or b., as appropriate, and c.*

a. *Individual or joint debtor(s) with primarily consumer debts:* List all payments on loans, installment purchases of goods or services, and other debts to any creditor made within 90 days immediately preceding the commencement of this case unless the aggregate value of all property that constitutes or is affected by such transfer is less than $600. Indicate with an asterisk (*) any payments that were made to a creditor on account of a domestic support obligation or as part of an alternative repayment schedule under a plan by an approved nonprofit budgeting and credit counseling agency. (Married debtors filing under chapter 12 or chapter 13 must include payments by either or both spouses whether or not a joint petition is filed, unless the spouses are separated and a joint petition is not filed.)

NAME AND ADDRESS OF CREDITOR	DATES OF PAYMENTS	AMOUNT PAID	AMOUNT STILL OWING
FSG Bank ATTN: Bankruptcy Dept. 4227 Ringgold Road East Ridge, TN 37421	January 2013	$1,250.00	$0.00

None ■ b. *Debtor whose debts are not primarily consumer debts:* List each payment or other transfer to any creditor made within 90 days immediately preceding the commencement of the case unless the aggregate value of all property that constitutes or is affected by such transfer is less than $5,850*. If the debtor is an individual, indicate with an asterisk (*) any payments that were made to a creditor on account of a domestic support obligation or as part of an alternative repayment schedule under a plan by an approved nonprofit budgeting and credit counseling agency. (Married debtors filing under chapter 12 or chapter 13 must include payments and other transfers by either or both spouses whether or not a joint petition is filed, unless the spouses are separated and a joint petition is not filed.)

NAME AND ADDRESS OF CREDITOR	DATES OF PAYMENTS/ TRANSFERS	AMOUNT PAID OR VALUE OF TRANSFERS	AMOUNT STILL OWING

None ■ c. *All debtors:* List all payments made within one year immediately preceding the commencement of this case to or for the benefit of creditors who are or were insiders. (Married debtors filing under chapter 12 or chapter 13 must include payments by either or both spouses whether or not a joint petition is filed, unless the spouses are separated and a joint petition is not filed.)

NAME AND ADDRESS OF CREDITOR AND RELATIONSHIP TO DEBTOR	DATE OF PAYMENT	AMOUNT PAID	AMOUNT STILL OWING

4. Suits and administrative proceedings, executions, garnishments and attachments

None ☐ a. List all suits and administrative proceedings to which the debtor is or was a party within one year immediately preceding the filing of this bankruptcy case. (Married debtors filing under chapter 12 or chapter 13 must include information concerning either or both spouses whether or not a joint petition is filed, unless the spouses are separated and a joint petition is not filed.)

CAPTION OF SUIT AND CASE NUMBER	NATURE OF PROCEEDING	COURT OR AGENCY AND LOCATION	STATUS OR DISPOSITION
Firstbank Vs. Sherrill Edward White, 10GS477	Suit on Account	In the Superior Court for the County of Catoosa	Pending
East Chattanooga Lumber & Supply Company Inc. vs Sherrill E. White amd Shirley White d/b/a SEW Construction Inc., 12-0066	Suit on Account	In the Chancery Court for the County of Hamilton, State of TN	Pending
USA Ready Mix			
S&M Building Supply			

* Amount subject to adjustment on 4/01/13, and every three years thereafter with respect to cases commenced on or after the date of adjustment.

- Section 3 asks for information about payments made to creditors within the 90 days preceding filing. The section is divided between consumer and nonconsumer debts. This is important because of the concept of fraudulent transfer. The trustee has to make sure that the debt payments were made within the ordinary course of business. Otherwise other creditors can claim that they were disadvantaged, arguing that the debtor knew he was going to file bankruptcy and intentionally shut them out.

- Section 4 requires the debtor to list all pending lawsuits.

B 7 (12/12)   3

CAPTION OF SUIT AND CASE NUMBER	NATURE OF PROCEEDING	COURT OR AGENCY AND LOCATION	STATUS OR DISPOSITION
Gateway Bank and Trust v. Sherrill White		Catoosa County Superior Court, State of GA	Pending

None ■   b. Describe all property that has been attached, garnished or seized under any legal or equitable process within one year immediately preceding the commencement of this case. (Married debtors filing under chapter 12 or chapter 13 must include information concerning property of either or both spouses whether or not a joint petition is filed, unless the spouses are separated and a joint petition is not filed.)

NAME AND ADDRESS OF PERSON FOR WHOSE BENEFIT PROPERTY WAS SEIZED	DATE OF SEIZURE	DESCRIPTION AND VALUE OF PROPERTY

5. Repossessions, foreclosures and returns

None □   List all property that has been repossessed by a creditor, sold at a foreclosure sale, transferred through a deed in lieu of foreclosure or returned to the seller, within one year immediately preceding the commencement of this case. (Married debtors filing under chapter 12 or chapter 13 must include information concerning property of either or both spouses whether or not a joint petition is filed, unless the spouses are separated and a joint petition is not filed.)

NAME AND ADDRESS OF CREDITOR OR SELLER	DATE OF REPOSSESSION, FORECLOSURE SALE, TRANSFER OR RETURN	DESCRIPTION AND VALUE OF PROPERTY
Gateway Bank P. O. Box 129 Ringgold, GA 30736	2012	Commercial Property located at 40 Savannah Way, Ft. Oglethorpe GA 30742

6. Assignments and receiverships

None ■   a. Describe any assignment of property for the benefit of creditors made within 120 days immediately preceding the commencement of this case. (Married debtors filing under chapter 12 or chapter 13 must include any assignment by either or both spouses whether or not a joint petition is filed, unless the spouses are separated and a joint petition is not filed.)

NAME AND ADDRESS OF ASSIGNEE	DATE OF ASSIGNMENT	TERMS OF ASSIGNMENT OR SETTLEMENT

None ■   b. List all property which has been in the hands of a custodian, receiver, or court-appointed official within one year immediately preceding the commencement of this case. (Married debtors filing under chapter 12 or chapter 13 must include information concerning property of either or both spouses whether or not a joint petition is filed, unless the spouses are separated and a joint petition is not filed.)

NAME AND ADDRESS OF CUSTODIAN	NAME AND LOCATION OF COURT CASE TITLE & NUMBER	DATE OF ORDER	DESCRIPTION AND VALUE OF PROPERTY

7. Gifts

None ■   List all gifts or charitable contributions made within one year immediately preceding the commencement of this case except ordinary and usual gifts to family members aggregating less than $200 in value per individual family member and charitable contributions aggregating less than $100 per recipient. (Married debtors filing under chapter 12 or chapter 13 must include gifts or contributions by either or both spouses whether or not a joint petition is filed, unless the spouses are separated and a joint petition is not filed.)

NAME AND ADDRESS OF PERSON OR ORGANIZATION	RELATIONSHIP TO DEBTOR, IF ANY	DATE OF GIFT	DESCRIPTION AND VALUE OF GIFT

- Section 5 asks the debtor to disclose any property that was recently seized or repossessed by creditors.
- Section 6 deals with receivership and assignment of property. The trustee is looking to see if the debtor has any property or money being held by third parties. This property, as well, is part of the bankruptcy estate.
- Section 7 asks about gifts. Again, this relates to fraudulent transfer. If ordinary, small, gifts are given for common purposes ($25 for a grandchild's birthday) it is of no concern. But if $10,000 is given for no good reason, that will cause the trustee to take action and demand the money back.

B 7 (12/12)   4

---

8. Losses

None
■   List all losses from fire, theft, other casualty or gambling within **one year** immediately preceding the commencement of this case **or since the commencement of this case.** (Married debtors filing under chapter 12 or chapter 13 must include losses by either or both spouses whether or not a joint petition is filed, unless the spouses are separated and a joint petition is not filed.)

DESCRIPTION AND VALUE OF PROPERTY	DESCRIPTION OF CIRCUMSTANCES AND, IF LOSS WAS COVERED IN WHOLE OR IN PART BY INSURANCE, GIVE PARTICULARS	DATE OF LOSS

---

9. Payments related to debt counseling or bankruptcy

None
☐   List all payments made or property transferred by or on behalf of the debtor to any persons, including attorneys, for consultation concerning debt consolidation, relief under the bankruptcy law or preparation of the petition in bankruptcy within **one year** immediately preceding the commencement of this case.

NAME AND ADDRESS OF PAYEE	DATE OF PAYMENT, NAME OF PAYOR IF OTHER THAN DEBTOR	AMOUNT OF MONEY OR DESCRIPTION AND VALUE OF PROPERTY
Greenpath Debt Solutions	2/26/13	35.00

---

10. Other transfers

None
☐   a. List all other property, other than property transferred in the ordinary course of the business or financial affairs of the debtor, transferred either absolutely or as security within **two years** immediately preceding the commencement of this case. (Married debtors filing under chapter 12 or chapter 13 must include transfers by either or both spouses whether or not a joint petition is filed, unless the spouses are separated and a joint petition is not filed.)

NAME AND ADDRESS OF TRANSFEREE, RELATIONSHIP TO DEBTOR	DATE	DESCRIBE PROPERTY TRANSFERRED AND VALUE RECEIVED
Suzette M. White	2005	Transferred House and 2 lots located at 337 Blue Jay Parkway, Chattanooga TN to daughter and Debtor's wife names
Daughter & Wife		
Savannah Springs, LLC	2012	LLC Sold Apartment Complex

None
■   b. List all property transferred by the debtor within **ten years** immediately preceding the commencement of this case to a self-settled trust or similar device of which the debtor is a beneficiary.

NAME OF TRUST OR OTHER DEVICE	DATE(S) OF TRANSFER(S)	AMOUNT OF MONEY OR DESCRIPTION AND VALUE OF PROPERTY OR DEBTOR'S INTEREST IN PROPERTY

---

11. Closed financial accounts

None
☐   List all financial accounts and instruments held in the name of the debtor or for the benefit of the debtor which were closed, sold, or otherwise transferred within **one year** immediately preceding the commencement of this case. Include checking, savings, or other financial accounts, certificates of deposit, or other instruments; shares and share accounts held in banks, credit unions, pension funds, cooperatives, associations, brokerage houses and other financial institutions. (Married debtors filing under chapter 12 or chapter 13 must include information concerning accounts or instruments held by or for either or both spouses whether or not a joint petition is filed, unless the spouses are separated and a joint petition is not filed.)

NAME AND ADDRESS OF INSTITUTION	TYPE OF ACCOUNT, LAST FOUR DIGITS OF ACCOUNT NUMBER, AND AMOUNT OF FINAL BALANCE	AMOUNT AND DATE OF SALE OR CLOSING
Northwest Georgia Bank P. O. Box 789 Ringgold, GA 30736	Savannah Springs Checking account was closed in Oct 2012 with a final balance being negative	Oct 2012

- Sections 8 through 11, continuing the theme of pre-bankruptcy distribution of funds, ask the debtor to disclose all other transfers of property or money, and also for information about closed bank accounts.

B 7 (12/12)

5

---

12. Safe deposit boxes

None
■

List each safe deposit or other box or depository in which the debtor has or had securities, cash, or other valuables within one year immediately preceding the commencement of this case. (Married debtors filing under chapter 12 or chapter 13 must include boxes or depositories of either or both spouses whether or not a joint petition is filed, unless the spouses are separated and a joint petition is not filed.)

NAME AND ADDRESS OF BANK OR OTHER DEPOSITORY	NAMES AND ADDRESSES OF THOSE WITH ACCESS TO BOX OR DEPOSITORY	DESCRIPTION OF CONTENTS	DATE OF TRANSFER OR SURRENDER, IF ANY

---

13. Setoffs

None
☐

List all setoffs made by any creditor, including a bank, against a debt or deposit of the debtor within 90 days preceding the commencement of this case. (Married debtors filing under chapter 12 or chapter 13 must include information concerning either or both spouses whether or not a joint petition is filed, unless the spouses are separated and a joint petition is not filed.)

NAME AND ADDRESS OF CREDITOR	DATE OF SETOFF	AMOUNT OF SETOFF
Northwest Georgia Bank P. O. Box 789 Ringgold, GA 30736	Northwest Georgia Bank has a hold on checking account.	

---

14. Property held for another person

None
■

List all property owned by another person that the debtor holds or controls.

NAME AND ADDRESS OF OWNER	DESCRIPTION AND VALUE OF PROPERTY	LOCATION OF PROPERTY

---

15. Prior address of debtor

None
■

If the debtor has moved within three years immediately preceding the commencement of this case, list all premises which the debtor occupied during that period and vacated prior to the commencement of this case. If a joint petition is filed, report also any separate address of either spouse.

ADDRESS	NAME USED	DATES OF OCCUPANCY

---

16. Spouses and Former Spouses

None
■

If the debtor resides or resided in a community property state, commonwealth, or territory (including Alaska, Arizona, California, Idaho, Louisiana, Nevada, New Mexico, Puerto Rico, Texas, Washington, or Wisconsin) within eight years immediately preceding the commencement of the case, identify the name of the debtor's spouse and of any former spouse who resides or resided with the debtor in the community property state.

NAME

---

17. Environmental Information.

For the purpose of this question, the following definitions apply:

"Environmental Law" means any federal, state, or local statute or regulation regulating pollution, contamination, releases of hazardous or toxic substances, wastes or material into the air, land, soil, surface water, groundwater, or other medium, including, but not limited to, statutes or regulations regulating the cleanup of these substances, wastes, or material.

"Site" means any location, facility, or property as defined under any Environmental Law, whether or not presently or formerly owned or operated by the debtor, including, but not limited to, disposal sites.

"Hazardous Material" means anything defined as a hazardous waste, hazardous substance, toxic substance, hazardous material, pollutant, or contaminant or similar term under an Environmental Law.

None
■

a. List the name and address of every site for which the debtor has received notice in writing by a governmental unit that it may be liable or potentially liable under or in violation of an Environmental Law. Indicate the governmental unit, the date of the notice, and, if known, the Environmental Law.

- Section 13 asks for setoffs, meaning claims that the debtor has against a creditor, which may reduce the debtor's liability to that creditor.
- The other sections ask for information about safe deposit boxes, prior addresses, and former spouses. This is only relevant in community property states.

Case 1:13-bk-11002   Doc 1   Filed 02/28/13   Entered 02/28/13 13:08:55   Desc Main
Document   Page 13 of 43

B 7 (13/12)   6

SITE NAME AND ADDRESS	NAME AND ADDRESS OF GOVERNMENTAL UNIT	DATE OF NOTICE	ENVIRONMENTAL LAW

None ■   b. List the name and address of every site for which the debtor provided notice to a governmental unit of a release of Hazardous Material. Indicate the governmental unit to which the notice was sent and the date of the notice.

SITE NAME AND ADDRESS	NAME AND ADDRESS OF GOVERNMENTAL UNIT	DATE OF NOTICE	ENVIRONMENTAL LAW

None ■   c. List all judicial or administrative proceedings, including settlements or orders, under any Environmental Law with respect to which the debtor is or was a party. Indicate the name and address of the governmental unit that is or was a party to the proceeding, and the docket number.

NAME AND ADDRESS OF GOVERNMENTAL UNIT	DOCKET NUMBER	STATUS OR DISPOSITION

18 . Nature, location and name of business

None ☐   a. *If the debtor is an individual*, list the names, addresses, taxpayer identification numbers, nature of the businesses, and beginning and ending dates of all businesses in which the debtor was an officer, director, partner, or managing executive of a corporation, partner in a partnership, sole proprietor, or was self-employed in a trade, profession, or other activity either full- or part-time within six years immediately preceding the commencement of this case, or in which the debtor owned 5 percent or more of the voting or equity securities within six years immediately preceding the commencement of this case.

If the debtor is a partnership, list the names, addresses, taxpayer identification numbers, nature of the businesses, and beginning and ending dates of all businesses in which the debtor was a partner or owned 5 percent or more of the voting or equity securities, within six years immediately preceding the commencement of this case.

If the debtor is a corporation, list the names, addresses, taxpayer identification numbers, nature of the businesses, and beginning and ending dates of all businesses in which the debtor was a partner or owned 5 percent or more of the voting or equity securities within six years immediately preceding the commencement of this case.

NAME	LAST FOUR DIGITS OF SOCIAL-SECURITY OR OTHER INDIVIDUAL TAXPAYER-I.D. NO. (ITIN)/ COMPLETE EIN	ADDRESS	NATURE OF BUSINESS	BEGINNING AND ENDING DATES
SEW Construction	45-0512403	302 Forest Avenue Chattanooga, TN 37401	Construction	2003-2008
Savannah Springs	582361029	35 Savannah Way Fort Oglethorpe, GA 30742	Apartments - 93 Units	1997-2012
Savannah Way	582497937	GA	Apartments - 10 units	1999-Current
KRW Partners/Suds and Shine	582534693	141 White Eagle Trail Chattanooga, TN 37421	Laundry Mat Business	2000-2012

None ■   b. Identify any business listed in response to subdivision a., above, that is "single asset real estate" as defined in 11 U.S.C. § 101.

NAME	ADDRESS

The following questions are to be completed by every debtor that is a corporation or partnership and by any individual debtor who is or has been, within six years immediately preceding the commencement of this case, any of the following: an officer, director, managing executive, or owner of more than 5 percent of the voting or equity securities of a corporation; a partner, other than a limited partner, of a partnership, a sole proprietor, or self-employed in a trade, profession, or other activity, either full- or part-time.

(An individual or joint debtor should complete this portion of the statement only if the debtor is or has been in business, as defined above, within six years immediately preceding the commencement of this case. A debtor who has not been in business within those six years should go directly to the signature page.)

- Section 18 here is key, as it will contain more detailed information about the debtor's businesses.

B 7 (12/12)   7

---

19. Books, records and financial statements

None ☐   a. List all bookkeepers and accountants who within two years immediately preceding the filing of this bankruptcy case kept or supervised the keeping of books of account and records of the debtor.

NAME AND ADDRESS	DATES SERVICES RENDERED
Hans Scmidt	2011, 2012
Chattanooga, TN 37421	

None ■   b. List all firms or individuals who within the two years immediately preceding the filing of this bankruptcy case have audited the books of account and records, or prepared a financial statement of the debtor.

NAME	ADDRESS	DATES SERVICES RENDERED

None ■   c. List all firms or individuals who at the time of the commencement of this case were in possession of the books of account and records of the debtor. If any of the books of account and records are not available, explain.

NAME	ADDRESS

None ■   d. List all financial institutions, creditors and other parties, including mercantile and trade agencies, to whom a financial statement was issued by the debtor within two years immediately preceding the commencement of this case.

NAME AND ADDRESS	DATE ISSUED

---

20. Inventories

None ■   a. List the dates of the last two inventories taken of your property, the name of the person who supervised the taking of each inventory, and the dollar amount and basis of each inventory.

DATE OF INVENTORY	INVENTORY SUPERVISOR	DOLLAR AMOUNT OF INVENTORY (Specify cost, market or other basis)

None ■   b. List the name and address of the person having possession of the records of each of the two inventories reported in a., above.

DATE OF INVENTORY	NAME AND ADDRESSES OF CUSTODIAN OF INVENTORY RECORDS

---

21. Current Partners, Officers, Directors and Shareholders

None ■   a. If the debtor is a partnership, list the nature and percentage of partnership interest of each member of the partnership.

NAME AND ADDRESS	NATURE OF INTEREST	PERCENTAGE OF INTEREST

None ■   b. If the debtor is a corporation, list all officers and directors of the corporation, and each stockholder who directly or indirectly owns, controls, or holds 5 percent or more of the voting or equity securities of the corporation.

NAME AND ADDRESS	TITLE	NATURE AND PERCENTAGE OF STOCK OWNERSHIP

---

22. Former partners, officers, directors and shareholders

None ☐   a. If the debtor is a partnership, list each member who withdrew from the partnership within one year immediately preceding the commencement of this case.

NAME	ADDRESS	DATE OF WITHDRAWAL
William Rench		Part of KRW Partners until the company was dissolved.
Dennis King	Ringgold, GA 30736	Was Partner in KRW Partners and Suds and Shine until the year of 2002

- These sections are devoted mostly to disclosure of business managers, executives, and partners.
- For certain creditors, Section 20 is important because it lists inventory. If you are trying to recover items held on consignment, or if you claim a lien on inventory, pay careful attention to this section.

B 7 (12/12)   8

| None ■ | b. If the debtor is a corporation, list all officers, or directors whose relationship with the corporation terminated within one year immediately preceding the commencement of this case. |

NAME AND ADDRESS	TITLE	DATE OF TERMINATION

23 . Withdrawals from a partnership or distributions by a corporation

| None ■ | If the debtor is a partnership or corporation, list all withdrawals or distributions credited or given to an insider, including compensation in any form, bonuses, loans, stock redemptions, options exercised and any other perquisite during one year immediately preceding the commencement of this case. |

NAME & ADDRESS OF RECIPIENT, RELATIONSHIP TO DEBTOR	DATE AND PURPOSE OF WITHDRAWAL	AMOUNT OF MONEY OR DESCRIPTION AND VALUE OF PROPERTY

24. Tax Consolidation Group.

| None ■ | If the debtor is a corporation, list the name and federal taxpayer identification number of the parent corporation of any consolidated group for tax purposes of which the debtor has been a member at any time within six years immediately preceding the commencement of the case. |

NAME OF PARENT CORPORATION	TAXPAYER IDENTIFICATION NUMBER (EIN)

25. Pension Funds.

| None ■ | If the debtor is not an individual, list the name and federal taxpayer-identification number of any pension fund to which the debtor, as an employer, has been responsible for contributing at any time within six years immediately preceding the commencement of the case. |

NAME OF PENSION FUND	TAXPAYER IDENTIFICATION NUMBER (EIN)

* * * * * *

- Note Section 23 on this page, which lists distributions to partners, officers, and shareholders. While here it is blank, it's a good place to catch questionable distributions of business funds.

B 7 (12/12)   9

DECLARATION UNDER PENALTY OF PERJURY BY INDIVIDUAL DEBTOR

I declare under penalty of perjury that I have read the answers contained in the foregoing statement of financial affairs and any attachments thereto and that they are true and correct.

Date February 28, 2013 _____   Signature   /s/ Sherrill Edward White _____
                                                          Sherrill Edward White
                                                          Debtor

Date February 28, 2013 _____   Signature   /s/ Shirley A. White _____
                                                          Shirley A. White
                                                          Joint Debtor

Penalty for making a false statement: Fine of up to $500,000 or imprisonment for up to 5 years, or both. 18 U.S.C. §§ 152 and 3571

- Again, this is just a signature page. But it is evidence of the debtor affirming everything in the Petition under penalty of perjury.

B6 Summary (Official Form 6 - Summary) (12/07)

United States Bankruptcy Court
Eastern District of Tennessee

In re   Sherrill Edward White,   Case No. _____
          Shirley A. White
_____   Chapter_____13_____
                                        Debtors

SUMMARY OF SCHEDULES

Indicate as to each schedule whether that schedule is attached and state the number of pages in each. Report the totals from Schedules A, B, D, E, F, I, and J in the boxes provided. Add the amounts from Schedules A and B to determine the total amount of the debtor's assets. Add the amounts of all claims from Schedules D, E, and F to determine the total amount of the debtor's liabilities. Individual debtors must also complete the "Statistical Summary of Certain Liabilities and Related Data" if they file a case under chapter 7, 11, or 13.

NAME OF SCHEDULE	ATTACHED (YES/NO)	NO. OF SHEETS	ASSETS	LIABILITIES	OTHER
A - Real Property	Yes	1	825,000.00		
B - Personal Property	Yes	4	15,107.66		
C - Property Claimed as Exempt	Yes	2			
D - Creditors Holding Secured Claims	Yes	1		1,016,663.00	
E - Creditors Holding Unsecured Priority Claims (Total of Claims on Schedule E)	Yes	1		0.00	
F - Creditors Holding Unsecured Nonpriority Claims	Yes	5		79,821.06	
G - Executory Contracts and Unexpired Leases	Yes	1			
H - Codebtors	Yes	1			
I - Current Income of Individual Debtor(s)	Yes	1			4,288.46
J - Current Expenditures of Individual Debtor(s)	Yes	1			4,077.00
Total Number of Sheets of ALL Schedules		18			
Total Assets			840,107.66		
Total Liabilities				1,096,484.06	

Software Copyright (c) 1996-2013 - CCH INCORPORATED - www.bestcase.com   Best Case Bankruptcy

- We begin the Schedules with the Summary of Schedules.
- This summarizes the assets and liabilities of the debtor. In a bankruptcy case, it should be inevitable that liabilities exceed assets.
- On this page, you can immediately spot red flags for missing assets, excessive or reduced claims of debt, or missing information.

Form 6 - Statistical Summary (12/07)

United States Bankruptcy Court
Eastern District of Tennessee

In re   Sherrill Edward White,   Case No. _____
          Shirley A. White

                                              Debtors   Chapter _____ 13 _____

STATISTICAL SUMMARY OF CERTAIN LIABILITIES AND RELATED DATA (28 U.S.C. § 159)

If you are an individual debtor whose debts are primarily consumer debts, as defined in § 101(8) of the Bankruptcy Code (11 U.S.C.§ 101(8)), filing a case under chapter 7, 11 or 13, you must report all information requested below.

☐ Check this box if you are an individual debtor whose debts are NOT primarily consumer debts. You are not required to report any information here.

This information is for statistical purposes only under 28 U.S.C. § 159.

Summarize the following types of liabilities, as reported in the Schedules, and total them.

Type of Liability	Amount
Domestic Support Obligations (from Schedule E)	0.00
Taxes and Certain Other Debts Owed to Governmental Units (from Schedule E)	0.00
Claims for Death or Personal Injury While Debtor Was Intoxicated (from Schedule E) (whether disputed or undisputed)	0.00
Student Loan Obligations (from Schedule F)	0.00
Domestic Support, Separation Agreement, and Divorce Decree Obligations Not Reported on Schedule E	0.00
Obligations to Pension or Profit-Sharing, and Other Similar Obligations (from Schedule F)	0.00
TOTAL	0.00

State the following:

Average Income (from Schedule I, Line 16)	4,288.46
Average Expenses (from Schedule J, Line 18)	4,077.00
Current Monthly Income (from Form 22A Line 12; OR, Form 22B Line 11; OR, Form 22C Line 20)	1,927.33

State the following:

1. Total from Schedule D, "UNSECURED PORTION, IF ANY" column		182,663.00
2. Total from Schedule E, "AMOUNT ENTITLED TO PRIORITY" column	0.00	
3. Total from Schedule E, "AMOUNT NOT ENTITLED TO PRIORITY, IF ANY" column		0.00
4. Total from Schedule F		79,821.06
5. Total of non-priority unsecured debt (sum of 1, 3, and 4)		262,484.06

- This Statistical Summary page factors income and unsecured debt into the bankruptcy calculation.

B6A (Official Form 6A) (12/07)

In re   Sherrill Edward White,   Case No. _____
         Shirley A. White
───
                Debtors
SCHEDULE A - REAL PROPERTY

Except as directed below, list all real property in which the debtor has any legal, equitable, or future interest, including all property owned as a cotenant, community property, or in which the debtor has a life estate. Include any property in which the debtor holds rights and powers exercisable for the debtor's own benefit. If the debtor is married, state whether husband, wife, both, or the marital community own the property by placing an "H," "W," "J," or "C" in the column labeled "Husband, Wife, Joint, or Community." If the debtor holds no interest in real property, write "None" under "Description and Location of Property."

Do not include interests in executory contracts and unexpired leases on this schedule. List them in Schedule G - Executory Contracts and Unexpired Leases.

If an entity claims to have a lien or hold a secured interest in any property, state the amount of the secured claim. See Schedule D. If no entity claims to hold a secured interest in the property, write "None" in the column labeled "Amount of Secured Claim." If the debtor is an individual or if a joint petition is filed, state the amount of any exemption claimed in the property only in Schedule C - Property Claimed as Exempt.

Description and Location of Property	Nature of Debtor's Interest in Property	Husband, Wife, Joint, or Community	Current Value of Debtor's Interest in Property, without Deducting any Secured Claim or Exemption	Amount of Secured Claim
Totally unfinished: House and acreage located at 2987 Salem Valley Road, Ringgold GA 30736 and Debtor's Residence: House and acreage located at 2989 Salem Valley Road, Ringgold GA 30736	Fee Simple	J	450,000.00	614,663.00
39, 43 Savannah Way, Ft. Oglethorpe GA 30742, 2 units	Fee Simple	J	375,000.00	390,000.00
13-45 Ashton Lane, Ft. Oglethorpe GA 30742, 8 units spread out				

Sub-Total >	825,000.00	(Total of this page)
Total >	825,000.00	
	(Report also on Summary of Schedules)	

__0__ continuation sheets attached to the Schedule of Real Property

Software Copyright (c) 1996-2013 - CCH INCORPORATED - www.bestcase.com   Best Case Bankruptcy

- Schedule A is a disclosure of all real property (real estate) in which the debtor has an interest. This includes all forms of ownership, but not leases.
- The debtor has to disclose the location of the property (address or legal description sufficient to identify the property), the nature of the property (house, raw land, commercial, industrial), the type of interest that he has (sole ownership, joint, fee simple, life estate), the value of the property, and the amount of claim that secured creditors have for debt owed encumbering the property.
- The value of the property has to be some form of market value.

Case 1:13-bk-11002   Doc 1   Filed 02/28/13   Entered 02/28/13 13:08:55   Desc Main
Document   Page 20 of 43

B6B (Official Form 6B) (12/07)

In re   Sherrill Edward White,   Case No. _____
Shirley A. White

Debtors

SCHEDULE B - PERSONAL PROPERTY

Except as directed below, list all personal property of the debtor of whatever kind. If the debtor has no property in one or more of the categories, place an "x" in the appropriate position in the column labeled "None." If additional space is needed in any category, attach a separate sheet properly identified with the case name, case number, and the number of the category. If the debtor is married, state whether husband, wife, both, or the marital community own the property by placing an "H," "W," "J," or "C" in the column labeled "Husband, Wife, Joint, or Community." If the debtor is an individual or a joint petition is filed, state the amount of any exemptions claimed only in Schedule C - Property Claimed as Exempt.

Do not list interests in executory contracts and unexpired leases on this schedule. List them in Schedule G - Executory Contracts and Unexpired Leases.

If the property is being held for the debtor by someone else, state that person's name and address under "Description and Location of Property." If the property is being held for a minor child, simply state the child's initials and the name and address of the child's parent or guardian, such as "A.B., a minor child, by John Doe, guardian." Do not disclose the child's name. See, 11 U.S.C. §112 and Fed. R. Bankr. P. 1007(m).

Type of Property	N O N E	Description and Location of Property	Husband, Wife, Joint, or Community	Current Value of Debtor's Interest in Property, without Deducting any Secured Claim or Exemption
1. Cash on hand	x			
2. Checking, savings or other financial accounts, certificates of deposit, or shares in banks, savings and loan, thrift, building and loan, and homestead associations, or credit unions, brokerage houses, or cooperatives.		Debtor's Checking account at Northwest Georgia Bank	J	400.00
		Joint Debtor's checking account at Northwest Georgia Bank	J	100.00
		Business checking for Savannah Way at Northwest GA Bank, Negative Balance	J	1.00
		Savings account at Met Comm Credit Union	J	1,200.00
3. Security deposits with public utilities, telephone companies, landlords, and others.	x			
4. Household goods and furnishings, including audio, video, and computer equipment.		Household Goods and Furnishings	J	2,000.00
5. Books, pictures and other art objects, antiques, stamp, coin, record, tape, compact disc, and other collections or collectibles.	x			
6. Wearing apparel.		Clothing and Apparel	J	300.00
7. Furs and jewelry.		Various Jewelry	J	1,000.00
8. Firearms and sports, photographic, and other hobby equipment.		Golf Clubs	J	100.00
		2 shotguns left to Debtor by Father	J	200.00
9. Interests in insurance policies. Name insurance company of each policy and itemize surrender or refund value of each.	x			

Sub-Total >   5,301.00
(Total of this page)

__3__ continuation sheets attached to the Schedule of Personal Property

Software Copyright (c) 1996-2013 - CCH INCORPORATED - www.bestcase.com   Best Case Bankruptcy

- Schedule B requires the debtor to list all of his personal property. This is everything that's not real estate.
- The form lists all of the different types of property. The debtor has to provide specific information about the property, his ownership interest, and the market value. Since used personal property usually has less value than new, these numbers will inevitably be low.
- One key point is that personal property has a lot of exemptions under state law, meaning that a debtor gets to keep the personal property they need to re-start their life after bankruptcy. But the exemption has limits. You will find that the values for the personal property conveniently coincide with the state exemption limits. There's nothing nefarious about this, as it is usually reasonably accurate. But it is something to take notice of if you know the debtor has some special property that they do not list.

B6B (Official Form 6B) (12/07) - Cont.

In re   **Sherrill Edward White,**   Case No. _____
           Shirley A. White

Debtors

SCHEDULE B - PERSONAL PROPERTY
(Continuation Sheet)

Type of Property	N O N E	Description and Location of Property	Husband, Wife, Joint, or Community	Current Value of Debtor's Interest in Property, without Deducting any Secured Claim or Exemption
10. Annuities. Itemize and name each issuer.	X			
11. Interests in an education IRA as defined in 26 U.S.C. § 530(b)(1) or under a qualified State tuition plan as defined in 26 U.S.C. § 529(b)(1). Give particulars. (File separately the record(s) of any such interest(s). 11 U.S.C. § 521(c).)	X			
12. Interests in IRA, ERISA, Keogh, or other pension or profit sharing plans. Give particulars.	X			
13. Stock and interests in incorporated and unincorporated businesses. Itemize.	X			
14. Interests in partnerships or joint ventures. Itemize.	X			
15. Government and corporate bonds and other negotiable and nonnegotiable instruments.	X			
16. Accounts receivable.		Debtor receives monthly interest payments of $305.66 from Valerie & Stephen Fraley for second mortgage. Set for 10 years starting in 2003 but they the Fraley's did not begin paying until approximately 2005.	J	305.66
		Debtor receives monthly interest on an unsecured promissory note from the sale of Savannah Springs in 2012. Maturity Date is 2017.	J	1.00
17. Alimony, maintenance, support, and property settlements to which the debtor is or may be entitled. Give particulars.	X			
18. Other liquidated debts owed to debtor including tax refunds. Give particulars.	X			
19. Equitable or future interests, life estates, and rights or powers exercisable for the benefit of the debtor other than those listed in Schedule A - Real Property.	X			
			Sub-Total > (Total of this page)	306.66

Sheet __1__ of __3__ continuation sheets attached
to the Schedule of Personal Property

- For business purposes, it's important to take note of Section 16 here and review accounts receivable. These accounts are an asset that can be assigned. Also, litigation can be instituted by the trustee on behalf of the estate.

B6B (Official Form 6B) (12/07) - Cont.

| In re | Sherrill Edward White, | Case No. _____ |
| | Shirley A. White | |

Debtors

SCHEDULE B - PERSONAL PROPERTY
(Continuation Sheet)

Type of Property	N O N E	Description and Location of Property	Husband, Wife, Joint, or Community	Current Value of Debtor's Interest in Property, without Deducting any Secured Claim or Exemption
20. Contingent and noncontingent interests in estate of a decedent, death benefit plan, life insurance policy, or trust.	X			
21. Other contingent and unliquidated claims of every nature, including tax refunds, counterclaims of the debtor, and rights to setoff claims. Give estimated value of each.	X			
22. Patents, copyrights, and other intellectual property. Give particulars.	X			
23. Licenses, franchises, and other general intangibles. Give particulars.	X			
24. Customer lists or other compilations containing personally identifiable information (as defined in 11 U.S.C. § 101(41A)) provided to the debtor by individuals in connection with obtaining a product or service from the debtor primarily for personal, family, or household purposes.	X			
25. Automobiles, trucks, trailers, and other vehicles and accessories.		2009 GMC Sierra, Approx 44,000 miles	J	9,000.00
		1995 Utility Trailer	J	500.00
26. Boats, motors, and accessories.	X			
27. Aircraft and accessories.	X			
28. Office equipment, furnishings, and supplies.	X			
29. Machinery, fixtures, equipment, and supplies used in business.	X			
30. Inventory.	X			
31. Animals.	X			
32. Crops - growing or harvested. Give particulars.	X			

Sub-Total >   9,500.00
(Total of this page)

Sheet __2__ of __3__ continuation sheets attached
to the Schedule of Personal Property

Software Copyright (c) 1996-2013 - CCH INCORPORATED - www.bestcase.com

Best Case Bankruptcy

- For businesses, look at equipment, machinery, and inventory. These may be assets, but they also may be encumbered by liens. If they're your liens, double check on the details and the value of these assets.

B6B (Official Form 6B) (12/07) - Cont.

In re   **Sherrill Edward White,**
         Shirley A. White   Case No. _____
_____
                                    Debtors

SCHEDULE B - PERSONAL PROPERTY
(Continuation Sheet)

Type of Property	N O N E	Description and Location of Property	Husband, Wife, Joint, or Community	Current Value of Debtor's Interest in Property, without Deducting any Secured Claim or Exemption
33. Farming equipment and implements.	X			
34. Farm supplies, chemicals, and feed.	X			
35. Other personal property of any kind not already listed. Itemize.	X			

Sub-Total > (Total of this page)	0.00
Total >	15,107.66

Sheet __3__ of __3__ continuation sheets attached
to the Schedule of Personal Property

(Report also on Summary of Schedules)

Software Copyright (c) 1996-2013 - CCH INCORPORATED - www.bestcase.com   Best Case Bankruptcy

- On the bottom of this page, you will see the total value of the personal property.

B6C (Official Form 6C) (4/10)

In re	Sherrill Edward White, Shirley A. White	Case No. _____
	Debtors	

SCHEDULE C - PROPERTY CLAIMED AS EXEMPT

Debtor claims the exemptions to which debtor is entitled under:
(Check one box)
☐ 11 U.S.C. §522(b)(2)
☒ 11 U.S.C. §522(b)(3)

☐ Check if debtor claims a homestead exemption that exceeds
$146,450. *(Amount subject to adjustment on 4/1/13, and every three years thereafter with respect to cases commenced on or after the date of adjustment.)*

Description of Property	Specify Law Providing Each Exemption	Value of Claimed Exemption	Current Value of Property Without Deducting Exemption
Real Property			
Totally unfinished: House and acreage located at 2987 Salem Valley Road, Ringgold GA 30736 and Debtor's Residence: House and acreage located at 2989 Salem Valley Road, Ringgold GA 30736	O.C.G.A. § 44-13-100(a)(1)	0.00	450,000.00
39, 43 Savannah Way, Ft. Oglethorpe GA 30742, 2 units	O.C.G.A. § 44-13-100(a)(1)	0.00	375,000.00
13-45 Ashton Lane, Ft. Oglethorpe GA 30742, 8 units spread out			
Checking, Savings, or Other Financial Accounts, Certificates of Deposit			
Debtor's Checking account at Northwest Georgia Bank	O.C.G.A. § 44-13-100(a)(6)	400.00	400.00
Joint Debtor's checking account at Northwest Georgia Bank	O.C.G.A. § 44-13-100(a)(6)	100.00	100.00
Business checking for Savannah Way at Northwest GA Bank, Negative Balance	O.C.G.A. § 44-13-100(a)(6)	1.00	1.00
Savings account at Met Comm Credit Union	O.C.G.A. § 44-13-100(a)(3)	1,200.00	1,200.00
Household Goods and Furnishings			
Household Goods and Furnishings	O.C.G.A. § 44-13-100(a)(4)	2,000.00	2,000.00
Wearing Apparel			
Clothing and Apparel	O.C.G.A. § 44-13-100(a)(4)	300.00	300.00
Furs and Jewelry			
Various Jewelry	O.C.G.A. § 44-13-100(a)(5)	1,000.00	1,000.00
Firearms and Sports, Photographic and Other Hobby Equipment			
Golf Clubs	O.C.G.A. § 44-13-100(a)(6)	100.00	100.00
2 shotguns left to Debtor by Father	O.C.G.A. § 44-13-100(a)(6)	200.00	200.00
Accounts Receivable			
Debtor receives monthly interest payments of $305.66 from Valerie & Stephen Fraley for second mortgage. Set for 10 years starting in 2003 but they the Fraley's did not begin paying until approximately 2005.	O.C.G.A. § 44-13-18	305.66	305.66
Debtor receives monthly interest on an unsecured promissory note from the sale of Savannah Springs in 2012. Maturity Date is 2017.	O.C.G.A. § 44-13-18	1.00	1.00

__1__ continuation sheets attached to Schedule of Property Claimed as Exempt

Software Copyright (C) 1996-2013 - CCH INCORPORATED - www.bestcase.com   Best Case Bankruptcy

- Schedule C lists the personal and real property exemptions. By state law, the debtor is allowed to claim a certain value of each type of property as exempt from liquidation.
- Review this list carefully to see if there is any excess value, meaning property that is worth more than the allowed exemption.

B6C (Official Form 6C) (4/10) – Cont.

In re   **Sherrill Edward White,**   Case No._____
         Shirley A. White
         _____
                          Debtors
              SCHEDULE C - PROPERTY CLAIMED AS EXEMPT
                          (Continuation Sheet)

Description of Property	Specify Law Providing Each Exemption	Value of Claimed Exemption	Current Value of Property Without Deducting Exemption
Automobiles, Trucks, Trailers, and Other Vehicles			
2009 GMC Sierra, Approx 44,000 miles	O.C.G.A. § 44-13-100(a)(3)	0.00	9,000.00
1995 Utility Trailer	O.C.G.A. § 44-13-100(a)(3)	500.00	500.00

| | Total: | 6,107.66 | 840,107.66 |

Sheet __1__ of __1__ continuation sheets attached to the Schedule of Property Claimed as Exempt

Software Copyright (c) 1996-2013 - CCH INCORPORATED - www.bestcase.com   Best Case Bankruptcy

- On the bottom of this page, you will find the amount of exempt property versus the total value of the property. If the latter is higher, there will be assets available for distribution to creditors.

Case 1:13-bk-11002 Doc 1 Filed 02/28/13 Entered 02/28/13 13:08:55 Desc Main
Document Page 26 of 43

B6D (Official Form 6D) (12/07)

In re **Sherrill Edward White,**
        Shirley A. White

Case No. _____

Debtors

SCHEDULE D - CREDITORS HOLDING SECURED CLAIMS

State the name, mailing address, including zip code, and last four digits of any account number of all entities holding claims secured by property of the debtor as of the date of filing of the petition. The complete account number of any account the debtor has with the creditor is useful to the trustee and the creditor and may be provided if the debtor chooses to do so. List creditors holding all types of secured interests such as judgment liens, garnishments, statutory liens, mortgages, deeds of trust, and other security interests.

List creditors in alphabetical order to the extent practicable. If a minor child is a creditor, the child's initials and the name and address of the child's parent or guardian, such as "A.B., a minor child, by John Doe, guardian." Do not disclose the child's name. See, 11 U.S.C. §112 and Fed. R. Bankr. P. 1007(m). If all secured creditors will not fit on this page, use the continuation sheet provided.

If any entity other than a spouse in a joint case may be jointly liable on a claim, place an "X" in the column labeled "Codebtor" include the entity on the appropriate schedule of creditors, and complete Schedule H - Codebtors. If a joint petition is filed, state whether the husband, wife, both of them, or the marital community may be liable on each claim by placing an "H", "W", "J", or "C" in the column labeled "Husband, Wife, Joint, or Community".

If the claim is contingent, place an "X" in the column labeled "Contingent". If the claim is unliquidated, place an "X" in the column labeled "Unliquidated". If the claim is disputed, place an "X" in the column labeled "Disputed". (You may need to place an "X" in more than one of these three columns.)

Total the columns labeled "Amount of Claim Without Deducting Value of Collateral" and "Unsecured Portion, if Any" in the boxes labeled "Total(s)" on the last sheet of the completed schedule. Report the total from the column labeled "Amount of Claim" also on the Summary of Schedules and, if the debtor is an individual with primarily consumer debts, report the total from the column labeled "Unsecured Portion" on the Statistical Summary of Certain Liabilities and Related Data.

☐ Check this box if debtor has no creditors holding secured claims to report on this Schedule D.

CREDITOR'S NAME AND MAILING ADDRESS INCLUDING ZIP CODE, AND ACCOUNT NUMBER (See instructions above.)	CODEBTOR	Husband, Wife, Joint, or Community		DATE CLAIM WAS INCURRED, NATURE OF LIEN, AND DESCRIPTION AND VALUE OF PROPERTY SUBJECT TO LIEN	CONTINGENT	UNLIQUIDATED	DISPUTED	AMOUNT OF CLAIM WITHOUT DEDUCTING VALUE OF COLLATERAL	UNSECURED PORTION, IF ANY
Account No.				Totally unfinished: House and acreage located at 2987 Salem Valley Road, Ringgold GA 30736 and Debtor's Residence: House and acreage located at 2989 Salem Valley Road, Ringgold GA 30736					
FSG Bank ATTN: Bankruptcy Dept. 531 Broad Street Chattanooga, TN 37402			J						
				Value $ 450,000.00				614,663.00	164,663.00
Account No.				39, 43 Savannah Way, Ft. Oglethorpe GA 30742, 2 units					
FSG Bank ATTN: Bankruptcy Dept. P. O. Box 11247 Chattanooga, TN 37401			J	13-45 Ashton Lane, Ft. Oglethorpe GA 30742, 8 units spread out					
				Value $ 375,000.00				390,000.00	15,000.00
Account No.				2009 GMC Sierra, Approx 44,000 miles					
MetCom Credit Union 17640 Highway 58 Decatur, TN			J						
				Value $ 9,000.00				12,000.00	3,000.00
Account No.									
				Value $					

__0__ continuation sheets attached

Subtotal (Total of this page)	1,016,663.00	182,663.00
Total (Report on Summary of Schedules)	1,016,663.00	182,663.00

Software Copyright (c) 1996-2013 - CCH INCORPORATED - www.bestcase.com

Best Case Bankruptcy

- Schedule D is a list of creditors holding secured claims on real and personal property.
- This schedule lists the name and address of the creditor, the property subject to the lien, the value of the property, and the amount of the lien claim.
- At the bottom will be the totals for lien claims versus value.
- If you believe you are a secured creditor but are not listed on Schedule D, it is important to bring that to the attention of your attorney immediately. Your attorney will inform the debtor's attorney and the trustee. Also make sure the numbers for your collateral are correct.

Case 1:13-bk-11002   Doc 1   Filed 02/28/13   Entered 02/28/13 13:08:55   Desc Main
Document   Page 27 of 43

B6E (Official Form 6E) (4/10)

In re   **Sherrill Edward White,**
Shirley A. White   Case No._____
                                        Debtors

SCHEDULE E - CREDITORS HOLDING UNSECURED PRIORITY CLAIMS

A complete list of claims entitled to priority, listed separately by type of priority, is to be set forth on the sheets provided. Only holders of unsecured claims entitled to priority should be listed in this schedule. In the boxes provided on the attached sheets, state the name, mailing address, including zip code, and last four digits of the account number, if any, of all entities holding priority claims against the debtor or the property of the debtor, as of the date of the filing of the petition. Use a separate continuation sheet for each type of priority and label each with the type of priority.

The complete account number of any account the debtor has with the creditor is useful to the trustee and the creditor and may be provided if the debtor chooses to do so. If a minor child is a creditor, state the child's initials and the name and address of the child's parent or guardian, such as "A.B., a minor child, by John Doe, guardian." Do not disclose the child's name. See, 11 U.S.C. §112 and Fed. R. Bankr. P. 1007(m).

If any entity other than a spouse in a joint case may be jointly liable on a claim, place an "X" in the column labeled "Codebtor," include the entity on the appropriate schedule of creditors, and complete Schedule H-Codebtors. If a joint petition is filed, state whether the husband, wife, both of them, or the marital community may be liable on each claim by placing an "H," "W," "J," or "C" in the column labeled "Husband, Wife, Joint, or Community." If the claim is contingent place an "X" in the column labeled "Contingent." If the claim is unliquidated, place an "X" in the column labeled "Unliquidated." If the claim is disputed, place an "X" in the column labeled "Disputed." (You may need to place an "X" in more than one of these three columns.)

Report the total of claims listed on each sheet in the box labeled "Subtotals" on each sheet. Report the total of all claims listed on this Schedule E in the box labeled "Total" on the last sheet of the completed schedule. Report this total also on the Summary of Schedules.

Report the total of amounts entitled to priority listed on each sheet in the box labeled "Subtotals" on each sheet. Report the total of all amounts entitled to priority listed on this Schedule E in the box labeled "Totals" on the last sheet of the completed schedule. Individual debtors with primarily consumer debts report this total also on the Statistical Summary of Certain Liabilities and Related Data.

Report the total of amounts not entitled to priority listed on each sheet in the box labeled "Subtotals" on each sheet. Report the total of all amounts not entitled to priority listed on this Schedule E in the box labeled "Totals" on the last sheet of the completed schedule. Individual debtors with primarily consumer debts report this total also on the Statistical Summary of Certain Liabilities and Related Data.

■ Check this box if debtor has no creditors holding unsecured priority claims to report on this Schedule E.

TYPES OF PRIORITY CLAIMS (Check the appropriate box(es) below if claims in that category are listed on the attached sheets)

☐ **Domestic support obligations**
Claims for domestic support that are owed to or recoverable by a spouse, former spouse, or child of the debtor, or the parent, legal guardian, or responsible relative of such a child, or a governmental unit to whom such a domestic support claim has been assigned to the extent provided in 11 U.S.C. § 507(a)(1).

☐ **Extensions of credit in an involuntary case**
Claims arising in the ordinary course of the debtor's business or financial affairs after the commencement of the case but before the earlier of the appointment of a trustee or the order for relief. 11 U.S.C. § 507(a)(3).

☐ **Wages, salaries, and commissions**
Wages, salaries, and commissions, including vacation, severance, and sick leave pay owing to employees and commissions owing to qualifying independent sales representatives up to $11,725* per person earned within 180 days immediately preceding the filing of the original petition, or the cessation of business, whichever occurred first, to the extent provided in 11 U.S.C. § 507(a)(4).

☐ **Contributions to employee benefit plans**
Money owed to employee benefit plans for services rendered within 180 days immediately preceding the filing of the original petition, or the cessation of business, whichever occurred first, to the extent provided in 11 U.S.C. § 507(a)(5).

☐ **Certain farmers and fishermen**
Claims of certain farmers and fishermen, up to $5,775* per farmer or fisherman, against the debtor, as provided in 11 U.S.C. § 507(a)(6).

☐ **Deposits by individuals**
Claims of individuals up to $2,600* for deposits for the purchase, lease, or rental of property or services for personal, family, or household use, that were not delivered or provided. 11 U.S.C. § 507(a)(7).

☐ **Taxes and certain other debts owed to governmental units**
Taxes, customs duties, and penalties owing to federal, state, and local governmental units as set forth in 11 U.S.C. § 507(a)(8).

☐ **Commitments to maintain the capital of an insured depository institution**
Claims based on commitments to the FDIC, RTC, Director of the Office of Thrift Supervision, Comptroller of the Currency, or Board of Governors of the Federal Reserve System, or their predecessors or successors, to maintain the capital of an insured depository institution. 11 U.S.C. § 507 (a)(9).

☐ **Claims for death or personal injury while debtor was intoxicated**
Claims for death or personal injury resulting from the operation of a motor vehicle or vessel while the debtor was intoxicated from using alcohol, a drug, or another substance. 11 U.S.C. § 507(a)(10).

* Amount subject to adjustment on 4/01/13, and every three years thereafter with respect to cases commenced on or after the date of adjustment

_____0_____ continuation sheets attached

Software Copyright (c) 1996-2013 - CCH INCORPORATED - www.bestcase.com   Best Case Bankruptcy

- Schedule E relates to unsecured priority claims. These are claims for child support, alimony, and taxes. Priority claims can also be salary and benefits owed to employees.

Case 1:13-bk-11002   Doc 1   Filed 02/28/13   Entered 02/28/13 13:08:55   Desc Main
Document   Page 28 of 43

B6F (Official Form 6F) (12/07)

In re   **Sherrill Edward White,**   Case No._____
Shirley A. White
_____
Debtors

SCHEDULE F - CREDITORS HOLDING UNSECURED NONPRIORITY CLAIMS

State the name, mailing address, including zip code, and last four digits of any account number, of all entities holding unsecured claims without priority against the debtor or the property of the debtor, as of the date of filing of the petition. The complete account number of any account the debtor has with the creditor is useful to the trustee and the creditor and may be provided if the debtor chooses to do so. If a minor child is a creditor, state the child's initials and the name and address of the child's parent or guardian, such as "A.B., a minor child, by John Doe, guardian." Do not disclose the child's name. See, 11 U.S.C. §112 and Fed. R. Bankr. P. 1007(m). Do not include claims listed in Schedules D and E. If all creditors will not fit on this page, use the continuation sheet provided.

If any entity other than a spouse in a joint case may be jointly liable on a claim, place an "X" in the column labeled "Codebtor," include the entity on the appropriate schedule of creditors, and complete Schedule H - Codebtors. If a joint petition is filed, state whether the husband, wife, both of them, or the marital community may be liable on each claim by placing an "H," "W," "J," or "C" in the column labeled "Husband, Wife, Joint, or Community."

If the claim is contingent, place an "X" in the column labeled "Contingent." If the claim is unliquidated, place an "X" in the column labeled "Unliquidated." If the claim is disputed, place an "X" in the column labeled "Disputed." (You may need to place an "X" in more than one of these three columns.)

Report the total of all claims listed on this schedule in the box labeled "Total" on the last sheet of the completed schedule. Report this total also on the Summary of Schedules and, if the debtor is an individual with primarily consumer debts, report this total also on the Statistical Summary of Certain Liabilities and Related Data.

☐   Check this box if debtor has no creditors holding unsecured claims to report on this Schedule F.

CREDITOR'S NAME, MAILING ADDRESS INCLUDING ZIP CODE, AND ACCOUNT NUMBER (See instructions above.)	CODEBTOR	Husband, Wife, Joint, or Community	DATE CLAIM WAS INCURRED AND CONSIDERATION FOR CLAIM. IF CLAIM IS SUBJECT TO SETOFF, SO STATE.	CONTINGENT	UNLIQUIDATED	DISPUTED	AMOUNT OF CLAIM
Account No. 120016245							
CACH LLC 4340 Monaco Street Second Floor Denver, CO 80237-3485		J					986.00
Account No.							
Community Trust & Banking 9125 Lee Highway Ooltewah, TN 37363		J					1.00
Account No.							
East Chattanooga Lumber c/o John Hull, Atty 801 Broad Street, Third Floor Pioneer Building Chattanooga, TN 37402		J					26,000.00
Account No.							
Enhanced Recovery Corporation 8014 Bayberry Road Jacksonville, FL 32256-7412		J					112.00
_4_ continuation sheets attached					Subtotal (Total of this page)		27,099.00

Software Copyright (c) 1996-2013 - CCH INCORPORATED - www.bestcase.com   S/N:25852-130118   Best Case Bankruptcy

- Schedule F lists unsecured, nonpriority claims. In other words, everyone else. Most unsecured creditors will be listed here.
- The schedule lists the name and address of the creditor, the date the debt was incurred (although it's rarely listed), and the amount of the claim.
- At the bottom you will find the total of the unsecured claims.
- Schedule F is usually multiple pages long. We show only the first page as an example.

B6G (Official Form 6G) (12/07)

In re   **Sherrill Edward White,**   Case No._____
         Shirley A. White
                                                    _____
                                                    Debtors

SCHEDULE G - EXECUTORY CONTRACTS AND UNEXPIRED LEASES

Describe all executory contracts of any nature and all unexpired leases of real or personal property. Include any timeshare interests. State nature
of debtor's interest in contract, i.e., "Purchaser", "Agent", etc. State whether debtor is the lessor or lessee of a lease. Provide the names and
complete mailing addresses of all other parties to each lease or contract described. If a minor child is a party to one of the leases or contracts,
state the child's initials and the name and address of the child's parent or guardian, such as "A.B., a minor child, by John Doe, guardian." Do not
disclose the child's name. See, 11 U.S.C. §112 and Fed. R. Bankr. P. 1007(m).

■ Check this box if debtor has no executory contracts or unexpired leases.

Name and Mailing Address, Including Zip Code, of Other Parties to Lease or Contract	Description of Contract or Lease and Nature of Debtor's Interest. State whether lease is for nonresidential real property. State contract number of any government contract.

0
____ continuation sheets attached to Schedule of Executory Contracts and Unexpired Leases

- Schedule G will list leases that are currently operative, along with other contracts that are ongoing at the time of bankruptcy.

B6H (Official Form 6H) (12/07)

In re   **Sherrill Edward White,**   Case No. _____
        Shirley A. White

Debtors

SCHEDULE H - CODEBTORS

Provide the information requested concerning any person or entity, other than a spouse in a joint case, that is also liable on any debts listed by debtor in the schedules of creditors. Include all guarantors and co-signers. If the debtor resides or resided in a community property state, commonwealth, or territory (including Alaska, Arizona, California, Idaho, Louisiana, Nevada, New Mexico, Puerto Rico, Texas, Washington, or Wisconsin) within the eight year period immediately preceding the commencement of the case, identify the name of the debtor's spouse and of any former spouse who resides or resided with the debtor in the community property state, commonwealth, or territory. Include all names used by the nondebtor spouse during the eight years immediately preceding the commencement of this case. If a minor child is a codebtor or a creditor, state the child's initials and the name and address of the child's parent or guardian, such as "A.B., a minor child, by John Doe, guardian." Do not disclose the child's name. See, 11 U.S.C. §112 and Fed. R. Bankr. P. 1007(m).

■ Check this box if debtor has no codebtors.

NAME AND ADDRESS OF CODEBTOR	NAME AND ADDRESS OF CREDITOR

0

_____ continuation sheets attached to Schedule of Codebtors

- Schedule H lists co-debtors. A co-debtor is a person or corporation obligated on a debt along with the debtor, but is not a party to the bankruptcy.

B6I (Official Form 6I) (12/07)

In re   **Sherrill Edward White**
        Shirley A. White   Case No. _____
                              Debtor(s)

SCHEDULE I - CURRENT INCOME OF INDIVIDUAL DEBTOR(S)

The column labeled "Spouse" must be completed in all cases filed by joint debtors and by every married debtor, whether or not a joint petition is filed, unless the spouses are separated and a joint petition is not filed. Do not state the name of any minor child. The average monthly income calculated on this form may differ from the current monthly income calculated on Form 22A, 22B, or 22C.

Debtor's Marital Status:	DEPENDENTS OF DEBTOR AND SPOUSE	
Married	RELATIONSHIP(S): None.	AGE(S):

Employment:	DEBTOR	SPOUSE
Occupation		
Name of Employer	Retired	Retired
How long employed		
Address of Employer		

INCOME: (Estimate of average or projected monthly income at time case filed)	DEBTOR	SPOUSE
1. Monthly gross wages, salary, and commissions (Prorate if not paid monthly)	$ 0.00	$ 0.00
2. Estimate monthly overtime	$ 0.00	$ 0.00
3. SUBTOTAL	$ 0.00	$ 0.00
4. LESS PAYROLL DEDUCTIONS		
a. Payroll taxes and social security	$ 0.00	$ 0.00
b. Insurance	$ 0.00	$ 0.00
c. Union dues	$ 0.00	$ 0.00
d. Other (Specify): _____	$ 0.00	$ 0.00
	$ 0.00	$ 0.00
5. SUBTOTAL OF PAYROLL DEDUCTIONS	$ 0.00	$ 0.00
6. TOTAL NET MONTHLY TAKE HOME PAY	$ 0.00	$ 0.00
7. Regular income from operation of business or profession or farm (Attach detailed statement)	$ 0.00	$ 0.00
8. Income from real property	$ 2,055.66	$ 0.00
9. Interest and dividends	$ 0.00	$ 0.00
10. Alimony, maintenance or support payments payable to the debtor for the debtor's use or that of dependents listed above	$ 0.00	$ 0.00
11. Social security or government assistance (Specify): **Monthly Social Security**	$ 1,482.80	$ 750.00
	$ 0.00	$ 0.00
12. Pension or retirement income	$ 0.00	$ 0.00
13. Other monthly income (Specify): _____	$ 0.00	$ 0.00
	$ 0.00	$ 0.00
14. SUBTOTAL OF LINES 7 THROUGH 13	$ 3,538.46	$ 750.00
15. AVERAGE MONTHLY INCOME (Add amounts shown on lines 6 and 14)	$ 3,538.46	$ 750.00
16. COMBINED AVERAGE MONTHLY INCOME: (Combine column totals from line 15)	$ 4,288.46	

(Report also on Summary of Schedules and, if applicable, on Statistical Summary of Certain Liabilities and Related Data)

17. Describe any increase or decrease in income reasonably anticipated to occur within the year following the filing of this document:
Debtor is interviewing for a part time position at Emerson Russell Properties. Has Verbal Agreement to be hired.

- Schedule I is a disclosure of the debtor's monthly living expenses. The purpose is to show that the debtor has enough income to meet his regular monthly living expenses, including debt payments, plus the Chapter 13 Plan payment on arrearages. In Chapter 7, this will show that the debtor does not have the ability to make his monthly payments and therefore should be granted a discharge.

- This schedule is pretty well scrutinized by the trustee. Often debtors will drastically overestimate or underestimate living expenses depending on their goal.

UNITED STATES BANKRUPTCY COURT
EASTERN DISTRICT OF TENNESSEE
NOTICE TO CONSUMER DEBTOR(S) UNDER § 342(b)
OF THE BANKRUPTCY CODE

In accordance with § 342(b) of the Bankruptcy Code, this notice to individuals with primarily consumer debts: (1) Describes briefly the services available from credit counseling services; (2) Describes briefly the purposes, benefits and costs of the four types of bankruptcy proceedings you may commence; and (3) Informs you about bankruptcy crimes and notifies you that the Attorney General may examine all information you supply in connection with a bankruptcy case.

You are cautioned that bankruptcy law is complicated and not easily described. Thus, you may wish to seek the advice of an attorney to learn of your rights and responsibilities should you decide to file a petition. Court employees cannot give you legal advice.

Notices from the bankruptcy court are sent to the mailing address you list on your bankruptcy petition. In order to ensure that you receive information about events concerning your case, Bankruptcy Rule 4002 requires that you notify the court of any changes in your address. If you are filing a joint case (a single bankruptcy case for two individuals married to each other), and each spouse lists the same mailing address on the bankruptcy petition, you and your spouse will generally receive a single copy of each notice mailed from the bankruptcy court in a jointly-addressed envelope, unless you file a statement with the court requesting that each spouse receive a separate copy of all notices.

1. Services Available from Credit Counseling Agencies

With limited exceptions, § 109(h) of the Bankruptcy Code requires that all individual debtors who file for bankruptcy relief on or after October 17, 2005, receive a briefing that outlines the available opportunities for credit counseling and provides assistance in performing a budget analysis. The briefing must be given within 180 days before the bankruptcy filing. The briefing may be provided individually or in a group (including briefings conducted by telephone or on the Internet) and must be provided by a nonprofit budget and credit counseling agency approved by the United States trustee or bankruptcy administrator. The clerk of the bankruptcy court has a list that you may consult of the approved budget and credit counseling agencies. Each debtor in a joint case must complete the briefing.

In addition, after filing a bankruptcy case, an individual debtor generally must complete a financial management instructional course before he or she can receive a discharge. The clerk also has a list of approved financial management instructional courses. Each debtor in a joint case must complete the course.

2. The Four Chapters of the Bankruptcy Code Available to Individual Consumer Debtors

Chapter 7: Liquidation ($245 filing fee, $46 administrative fee, $15 trustee surcharge: Total Fee $306)

Chapter 7 is designed for debtors in financial difficulty who do not have the ability to pay their existing debts. Debtors whose debts are primarily consumer debts are subject to a "means test" designed to determine whether the case should be permitted to proceed under chapter 7. If your income is greater than the median income for your state of residence and family size, in some cases, the United States trustee (or bankruptcy administrator), the trustee, or creditors have the right to file a motion requesting that the court dismiss your case under § 707(b) of the Code. It is up to the court to decide whether the case should be dismissed.

Under chapter 7, you may claim certain of your property as exempt under governing law. A trustee may have the right to take possession of and sell the remaining property that is not exempt and use the sale proceeds to pay your creditors.

The purpose of filing a chapter 7 case is to obtain a discharge of your existing debts. If, however, you are found to have committed certain kinds of improper conduct described in the Bankruptcy Code, the court may deny your discharge and, if it does, the purpose for which you filed the bankruptcy petition will be defeated.

Even if you receive a general discharge, some particular debts are not discharged under the law. Therefore, you may still be responsible for most taxes and student loans; debts incurred to pay nondischargeable taxes; domestic support and property settlement obligations; most fines, penalties, forfeitures, and criminal restitution obligations; certain debts which are not properly listed in your bankruptcy papers; and debts for death or personal injury caused by operating a motor vehicle, vessel, or aircraft while intoxicated from alcohol or drugs. Also, if a creditor can prove that a debt arose from fraud, breach of fiduciary duty, or theft, or from a willful and malicious injury, the bankruptcy court may determine that the debt is not discharged.

Chapter 13: Repayment of All or Part of the Debts of an Individual with Regular Income ($235 filing fee, $46 administrative fee: Total fee $281)

Chapter 13 is designed for individuals with regular income who would like to pay all or part of their debts in installments over

- This disclosure is provided to the debtor pursuant to the bankruptcy code. It is a "plain English" summary of the bankruptcy laws so the debtor will understand their obligations and what they're getting themselves into. I present it here so you understand bankruptcy from the debtor's perspective. The debtor certifies that they've read this form before filing for bankruptcy protection.

Form B 201A. Notice to Consumer Debtor(s)   Page 2

a period of time. You are only eligible for chapter 13 if your debts do not exceed certain dollar amounts set forth in the Bankruptcy Code.

Under chapter 13, you must file with the court a plan to repay your creditors all or part of the money that you owe them, using your future earnings. The period allowed by the court to repay your debts may be three years or five years, depending upon your income and other factors. The court must approve your plan before it can take effect.

After completing the payments under your plan, your debts are generally discharged except for domestic support obligations; most student loans; certain taxes; most criminal fines and restitution obligations; certain debts which are not properly listed in your bankruptcy papers; certain debts for acts that caused death or personal injury; and certain long term secured obligations.

Chapter 11: Reorganization ($1,167 filing fee, $46 administrative fee: Total fee $1,213)

Chapter 11 is designed for the reorganization of a business but is also available to consumer debtors. Its provisions are quite complicated, and any decision by an individual to file a chapter 11 petition should be reviewed with an attorney.

Chapter 12: Family Farmer or Fisherman ($200 filing fee, $46 administrative fee: Total fee $246)

Chapter 12 is designed to permit family farmers and fishermen to repay their debts over a period of time from future earnings and is similar to chapter 13. The eligibility requirements are restrictive, limiting its use to those whose income arises primarily from a family-owned farm or commercial fishing operation.

3. Bankruptcy Crimes and Availability of Bankruptcy Papers to Law Enforcement Officials

A person who knowingly and fraudulently conceals assets or makes a false oath or statement under penalty of perjury, either orally or in writing, in connection with a bankruptcy case is subject to a fine, imprisonment, or both. All information supplied by a debtor in connection with a bankruptcy case is subject to examination by the Attorney General acting through the Office of the United States Trustee, the Office of the United States Attorney, and other components and employees of the Department of Justice.

WARNING: Section 521(a)(1) of the Bankruptcy Code requires that you promptly file detailed information regarding your creditors, assets, liabilities, income, expenses and general financial condition. Your bankruptcy case may be dismissed if this information is not filed with the court within the time deadlines set by the Bankruptcy Code, the Bankruptcy Rules, and the local rules of the court. The documents and the deadlines for filing them are listed on Form B200, which is posted at http://www.uscourts.gov/bkforms/bankruptcy_forms.html#procedure.

- This is the second page of the required disclosure.

```
CACH LLC
4340 Monaco Street
Second Floor
Denver, CO 80237-3485

Community Trust & Banking
9125 Lee Highway
Ooltewah, TN 37363

East Chattanooga Lumber
c/o John Hull, Atty
801 Broad Street, Third Floor
Pioneer Building
Chattanooga, TN 37402

Enhanced Recovery Corporation
8014 Bayberry Road
Jacksonville, FL 32256-7412

Firstbank
c/o Douglas Brooks
PO Box 8477
Atlanta, GA 31106

FSG Bank
ATTN: Bankruptcy Dept.
531 Broad Street
Chattanooga, TN 37402

FSG Bank
ATTN: Bankruptcy Dept.
P. O. Box 11247
Chattanooga, TN 37401

Gateway Bank
P. O. Box 129
Ringgold, GA 30736

GMAC Auto Financing
PO Box 380901
Minneapolis, MN 55438

Griff Shirley
c/o William Slack Attorney
108 E. Lafayette Square
La Fayette, GA 30728

Home Depot
PO Box 653000
Dallas, TX 75265-3000

Home Depot Credit Services
P.O. Box 6497
Sioux Falls, SD 57117-6497
```

- The Petition and Schedules concludes with a mailing list of all the creditors. Review the list and see who else the debtor has business with. This could provide insight into how they got into bankruptcy and how assets may be distributed.

Chapter 13 Debtor's Plan of Reorganization

The Chapter 13 Plan is the debtor's proposal to pay off pre-petition accrued debt to secured creditors (the arrearage), while maintaining payments on other debts secured by property that the debtor intends to keep, and also keeping up with their living expenses. The following is an example of a Chapter 13 Plan. We'll go through it in detail so you can identify where your business might fit into the plan, and where you should be concerned. Discussing the plan in detail with your attorney is the best way to understand the impact of a Chapter 13 Plan on your business. Unlike the Petition, which is a standard form across the country, the form of the Plan may differ by district. But the essential points are the same. The plan shown here is from the Northern District of Georgia, which tends to be lengthy.

Case 12-23825-reb   Doc 2   Filed 11/05/12   Entered 11/05/12 12:30:25   Desc Main
Document   Page 1 of 5

United States Bankruptcy Court
NORTHERN DISTRICT OF GEORGIA - GAINESVILLE DIVISION

In re   **William Eimple Delaney** _____   Case No. _____
_____
Debtor(s)   Chapter   13

CHAPTER 13 PLAN

Extension ☒   Composition ☐

　　　You should read this Plan carefully and discuss it with your attorney. Confirmation of this Plan by the Bankruptcy Court may modify your rights by providing for payment of less than the full amount of your claim, by setting the value of the collateral securing your claim, and/or by setting the interest rate on your claim.

Debtor or Debtors (hereinafter called "Debtor") proposes this Chapter 13 Plan:

1. **Submission of Income.** Debtor submits to the supervision and control of the Chapter 13 Trustee ("Trustee") all or such portion of future earnings or other future income of Debtor as is necessary for the execution of this Plan.

2. **Plan Payments and Length of Plan.** Debtor will pay the sum of __$1,500.00_ **Monthly**_ to Trustee by ☐ Payroll Deduction(s) or by ☒ Direct Payment(s) for the applicable commitment period of _36_ months, unless all allowed claims in every class, other than long-term claims, are paid in full in a shorter period of time. The term of this Plan shall not exceed sixty (60) months. *See* 11 U.S.C. §§ 1325(b)(1)(B) and 1325(b)(4). Each pre-confirmation plan payment shall be reduced by any pre-confirmation adequate protection payment(s) made pursuant to Plan paragraph 6(A)(i) and § 1326(a)(1)(C).

　　The following alternative provision will apply if selected:

　　　☐ IF CHECKED, Plan payments will increase by $__ in month __ upon completion or termination of __.

3. **Claims Generally. The amounts listed for claims in this Plan are based upon Debtor's best estimate and belief.** An allowed proof of claim will be controlling, unless the Court orders otherwise. Objections to claims may be filed before or after confirmation.

4. **Administrative Claims.** Trustee will pay in full allowed administrative claims and expenses pursuant to §507(a)(2) as set forth below, unless the holder of such claim or expense has agreed to a different treatment of its claim.

　　(A). **Trustee's Fees.** Trustee shall receive a fee for each disbursement, the percentage of which is fixed by the United States Trustee.

　　(B). **Debtor's Attorney's Fees.** Debtor and Debtor's attorney have agreed to a base attorney fee in the amount of $__6,500.00__ for the services identified in the Rule 2016(b) disclosure statement filed in this case. The amount of $__0.00__ was paid prior to the filing of the case. The balance of the fee shall be disbursed by Trustee as follows: (1) Upon the first disbursement of the plan following confirmation of a Plan, the Trustee shall disburse to Debtor's attorney from the proceeds available and paid into the office of the Trustee by Debtor or on Debtor's behalf, up to $__6,500.00__ after the payment of adequate protection payments and administrative fees. The remaining balance of the fees shall be paid up to $__1,000.00__ per month until the fees are paid in full; (2) If the case is dismissed or converted prior to confirmation of the plan, the Trustee shall pay fees to Debtor's attorney from the proceeds available and paid into the office of the Trustee by Debtor or on Debtor's behalf, all funds remaining, not to exceed $__6,500.00__, after payment of any unpaid filing fees, Trustee's fees and expenses, and adequate protection payments, if applicable.

5. **Priority Claims.**

　　(A). **Domestic Support Obligations.**

☒ None. If none, skip to Plan paragraph 5(B).

　　　(i). Debtor is required to pay all post-petition domestic support obligations directly to the holder of the claim.

1

Software Copyright (c) 1996-2012 CCH INCORPORATED - www.bestcase.com

04.14.08

Best Case Bankruptcy

- The key parts of the Plan are anything that involves filling in the blanks, or adding text. Note Section 2, which sets out the monthly Chapter 13 Plan payment, how the payment will be made (whether directly to creditors or to the trustee), and Section 4, which is the debtor's attorney's fee.

- If the monthly Plan payment, plus monthly expenses, exceeds monthly income then the Plan is not feasible and has to be revised.

- The attorney's fee is subject to the trustee's review for being excessive. Most attorneys stay within the bounds of local custom on this matter.

Case 12-23825-reb   Doc 2   Filed 11/05/12   Entered 11/05/12 12:30:25   Desc Main
Document   Page 2 of 5

(ii). The name(s) and address(es) of the holder of any domestic support obligation are as follows. *See* 11 U.S.C. §§ 101(14A) and 1302(b)(6).

> -NONE-

(iii). Anticipated Domestic Support Obligation Arrearage Claims

(a). Unless otherwise specified in this Plan, priority claims under 11 U.S.C. § 507(a)(1) will be paid in full pursuant to 11 U.S.C. § 1322(a)(2). These claims will be paid at the same time as claims secured by personal property, arrearage claims secured by real property, and arrearage claims for assumed leases or executory contracts.

☒ None; or

(a) Creditor (Name and Address)	(b) Estimated arrearage claim	(c) Projected monthly arrearage payment
-NONE-		

(b). Pursuant to §§ 507(a)(1)(B) and 1322(a)(4), the following domestic support obligation claims are assigned to, owed to, or recoverable by a governmental unit.

☒ None; or

Claimant and proposed treatment: -NONE-_____

(B). Other Priority Claims (e.g., tax claims). All other allowed priority claims will be paid in full, but will not be funded until after all secured claims, lease arrearage claims, and domestic support claims are paid in full.

(a) Creditor	(b) Estimated claim
Georgia Department of Revenue	12,000.00
IRS	2,135.00

6. Secured Claims.

(A). Claims Secured by Personal Property Which Debtor Intends to Retain.

(i). **Pre-confirmation adequate protection payments.** No later than 30 days after the date of filing of this plan or the order for relief, whichever is earlier, the Debtor shall make the following adequate protection payments to creditors pursuant to § 1326(a)(1)(C). If the Debtor elects to make such adequate protection payments on allowed claims to the Trustee pending confirmation of the plan, the creditor shall have an administrative lien on such payment(s), subject to objection. If Debtor elects to make such adequate protection payments directly to the creditor, Debtor shall provide evidence of such payment to the Trustee, including the amount and date of the payment.

Debtor shall make the following adequate protection payments:

☐ directly to the creditor; or

☒ to the Trustee pending confirmation of the plan.

(a) Creditor	(b) Collateral	(c) Adequate protection payment amount
-NONE-		

(ii). **Post confirmation payments.** Post-confirmation payments to creditors holding claims secured by personal property

2   04.14.08

- On this page, note the priority claims of taxes. Taxes can include unpaid income or payroll taxes due to the federal government or the state. Taxes can also include unpaid property taxes.

- The Plan requires that pre-confirmation payments be made, known as "adequate protection." This page notes whether special pre-confirmation payments will be made or whether payments will be made through the trustee under the regular terms of the Plan.

- A creditor can claim that the payments are "inadequate" if they do not lead to the arrearage being paid off by the end of the term of the Plan, among other reasons.

Case 12-23825-reb   Doc 2   Filed 11/05/12   Entered 11/05/12 12:30:25   Desc Main
Document   Page 3 of 5

shall be paid as set forth in subparagraphs (a) and (b). If the Debtor elects to propose a different method of payment, such provision is set forth in paragraph (c).

(a). **Claims to Which § 506 Valuation is NOT Applicable.** Claims listed in this subsection consist of debts secured by a purchase money security interest in a vehicle for which the debt was incurred within 910 days of filing the bankruptcy petition, or, if the collateral for the debt is any other thing of value, the debt was incurred within 1 year of filing. *See* § 1325(a)(5). After confirmation of the plan, the Trustee will pay to the holder of each allowed secured claim the monthly payment in column (f) based upon the amount of the claim in column (d) with interest at the rate stated in column (e). Upon confirmation of the plan, the interest rate shown below or as modified will be binding unless a timely written objection to confirmation is filed and sustained by the Court. Payments distributed by the Trustee are subject to the availability of funds.

☒ None; or

(a) Creditor	(b) Collateral	(c) Purchase date	(d) Claim amount	(e) Interest rate	(f) Monthly payment
-NONE-					

(b). **Claims to Which § 506 Valuation is Applicable.** Claims listed in this subsection consist of any claims secured by personal property not described in Plan paragraph 6(A)(ii)(a). After confirmation of the plan, the Trustee will pay to the holder of each allowed secured claim the monthly payment in column (f) based upon the replacement value as stated in column (d) or the amount of the claim, whichever is less, with interest at the rate stated in column (e). The portion of any allowed claim that exceeds the value indicated below will be treated as an unsecured claim. Upon confirmation of the plan, the valuation and interest rate shown below or as modified will be binding unless a timely written objection to confirmation is filed and sustained by the Court. Payments distributed by the Trustee are subject to the availability of funds.

☐ None; or

(a) Creditor	(b) Collateral	(c) Purchase date	(d) Replacement value	(e) Interest rate	(f) Monthly payment
Willie Thurmond	Vacant Lot of 2 Acres on Barber Creek Road Parcel Number XX132 037 Statham, GA 30666		14,445.00(anticipated claim $10,000.00)	3.00%	$300.00

(c). **Other provisions.**

3

04.14.08

Software Copyright (c) 1996-2012 CCH INCORPORATED - www.bestcase.com

Best Case Bankruptcy

- This page will contain Plan information for personal property. The debtor will list the personal property that is collateral for loans, and his intent for retaining or abandoning the property.
- If the debtor is going to keep the property, he has to set out the repayment plan for the arrearage. It must totally pay off the arrearage, but the interest rate must be high enough to be "adequate" but low enough that the debtor can afford the payment.
- This debtor made an error listing real property here.

Case 12-23825-reb   Doc 2   Filed 11/05/12   Entered 11/05/12 12:30:25   Desc Main
Document   Page 4 of 5

(B). **Claims Secured by Real Property Which Debtor Intends to Retain.** Debtor will make all post-petition mortgage payments directly to each mortgage creditor as those payments ordinarily come due. These regular monthly mortgage payments, which may be adjusted up or down as provided for under the loan documents, are due beginning the first due date after the case is filed and continuing each month thereafter, unless this Plan provides otherwise. Trustee may pay each allowed arrearage claim at the monthly rate indicated below until paid in full. Trustee will pay interest on the mortgage arrearage if the creditor requests interest, unless an objection to the claim is filed and an order is entered disallowing the requested interest.

(a) Creditor	(b) Property description	(c) Estimated pre-petition arrearage	(d) Projected monthly arrearage payment
Barrow County Tax Assessor	Additional Property 596 8th Street Statham, GA 30666	1,000.00	$50.00 beginning June 2013
Barrow County Tax Assessor	Additional Property 8th Street Statham, GA 30666	1,000.00	$50.00 beginning June 2013
Barrow County Tax Assessor	Vacant Lot Highway 316 21.43 Acres	1,000.00	$50.00 beginning June 2013
Barrow County Tax Assessor	Additional Property 610 Barber Creek Road Statham, GA 30666	1,000.00	$50.00 beginning June 2013
Southern Community Bank	583, 585, 593 Eighth Street, Statham, GA 30666	15,000.00	$490.00 beginning June 2013
Southern Community Bank	Residence 616 Barber Creek Road Statham, GA 30666	15,000.00	$490.00 beginning June 2013

(C). **Surrender of Collateral.** Debtor will surrender the following collateral no later than thirty (30) days from the filing of the petition unless specified otherwise in the Plan. Any claim filed by a secured lien holder whose collateral is surrendered will be treated as unsecured. Any involuntary repossession/foreclosure prior to confirmation of this Plan must be obtained by a filed motion and Court order, unless the automatic stay no longer applies under § 362(c). Upon Plan confirmation, the automatic stay will be deemed lifted for the collateral identified below for surrender and the creditor need not file a Motion to Lift the Stay in order to repossess, foreclose upon or sell the collateral. Nothing herein is intended to lift any applicable co-Debtor stay, or to abrogate Debtor's state law contract rights.

(a) Creditor	(b) Collateral to be surrendered
-NONE-	

7. **Unsecured Claims.** Debtor estimates that the total of general unsecured debt not separately classified in Plan paragraph 10 is $ _15,115.00_ . After all other classes have been paid, Trustee will pay to the creditors with allowed general unsecured claims a pro rata share of $ _0.00_ or _100_ %, whichever is greater. Trustee is authorized to increase this dollar amount or percentage, if necessary, in order to comply with the applicable commitment period stated in paragraph 2 of this Plan.

8. **Executory Contracts and Unexpired Leases.** The following executory contracts and unexpired leases are assumed, and payments due after the filing of the case will be paid directly by Debtor, not through Trustee, as set forth below in column (c).

Debtor proposes to cure any default by paying the arrearage on the assumed leases or contracts in the amounts projected in column (d) at the same time that payments are made to secured creditors. All other executory contracts and unexpired leases of personal property are rejected upon conclusion of the confirmation hearing.

☒ None; or

(a) Creditor	(b) Nature of lease or executory contract	(c) Payment to be paid directly by Debtor	(d) Projected arrearage monthly payment through plan (for informational purposes)
-NONE-			

9. **Property of the Estate.** Property of the estate shall not vest in Debtor until the earlier of Debtor's discharge or dismissal of this case, unless the Court orders otherwise.

4   04.14.08

- This page relates to real property. The debtor has to list all of his encumbered real property and declare what he intends to retain and let go.
- If he is going to retain the real property, he has to state how he will pay off the arrearage. Just as previously, the arrearage payment must be feasible given his income and expenses.
- This page also lists unsecured claims and whether unsecured creditors will realize any payment from the Plan. In most cases, the answer is "no."

10. **Other Provisions**:

    (A). **Special classes of unsecured claims**.

    (B). **Other direct payments to creditors**.

    (C). **Other allowed secured claims**: A proof of claim which is filed and allowed as a secured claim, but is not treated specifically under the plan, shall be funded with **3** % interest as funds become available after satisfaction of the allowed secured claims which have been treated by the plan and prior to payment of allowed non-administrative priority claims (except domestic support obligation claims as set forth in paragraph 5(A), above) and general unsecured claims. Notwithstanding the foregoing, the Debtor or any other party in interest may object to the allowance of the claim.

    (D). **Claims subject to lien avoidance pursuant to 11 U.S.C. §522(f)**: The allowed secured claim of each creditor listed below shall not be funded until all allowed, secured claims which are being treated by the plan are satisfied. If an order is entered avoiding the creditor's lien, that creditor's claim shall be treated as a general, unsecured claim to the extent it is not otherwise secured by property of the estate and treated by the plan. To the extent that the creditor's lien is not avoided and is not otherwise treated by the plan, the secured claim shall be funded as set forth in the above paragraph. This paragraph shall apply to the following creditors:
    -NONE-

Date November 5, 2012   Signature /s/ William Eimple Delaney
                                             William Eimple Delaney
                                             Debtor

Attorney /s/ Kelsea L. S. Laun, GA Bar No.
            Kelsea L. S. Laun, GA Bar No. 141960
            Clark & Washington, LLC
            3300 NE Expressway
            Building 3
            Atlanta, GA 30341
            (404) 522-2222
            (770) 220-0685 - fax

04.14.08

Best Case Bankruptcy

- Pay careful attention to the "Other Provisions" on this page. While it is blank here, often this is where debtors sneak in provisions that are not to the liking of secured creditors. They may say that payments will be one amount initially and another amount later. It's also common to list intentions to strip an inferior lien or mortgage at this point.
- If that is the case, speak to your attorney about rvemedies to preserve your lien rights and chance at receiving payment.

Creditor's Proof of Claim

A creditor files a Proof of Claim to let the trustee, the debtor, and other creditors know the amount and nature of their claim. The Proof of Claim is used to establish security status and priority when payments are being made. In most cases, a Proof of Claim is only filed in a Chapter 13 case. But sometimes, if a Chapter 7 case has assets to be distributed, the trustee will direct creditors to file a Proof of Claim. The following is an example of a Proof of Claim. If the claim is secured, most districts require a copy of the security agreement to be included with the filing, such as a mortgage, deed of trust, security deed, or UCC-1 statement. Some districts allow businesses and corporate entities to file their own Proofs of Claim. Others require an attorney to file on behalf of a corporation. Either way, let's review the required information so you can fill it out on your own behalf, or assist your attorney more effectively.

B10 (Official Form 10) (04/13)

UNITED STATES BANKRUPTCY COURT Southern District of Georgia		PROOF OF CLAIM
Name of Debtor: JOHN MELCHER FORD	Case Number: 12-21364-JSD	

NOTE: *Do not use this form to make a claim for an administrative expense that arises after the bankruptcy filing. You may file a request for payment of an administrative expense according to 11 U.S.C. § 503.*

Name of Creditor (the person or other entity to whom the debtor owes money or property):
State Bank and Trust

Name and address where notices should be sent:
c/o Busch, Slipakoff & Schuh, LLP
3330 Cumberland Blvd, Suite 300
Atlanta, Georgia 30339

Telephone number: (770) 790-3550   email: skuperberg@bssfirm.com

Name and address where payment should be sent (if different from above):

Telephone number: email:

COURT USE ONLY

☐ Check this box if this claim amends a previously filed claim.

Court Claim Number:_____
(if known)

Filed on:_____

☐ Check this box if you are aware that anyone else has filed a proof of claim relating to this claim. Attach copy of statement giving particulars.

1. Amount of Claim as of Date Case Filed: $ 535,000.00

If all or part of the claim is secured, complete item 4.

If all or part of the claim is entitled to priority, complete item 5.

☐ Check this box if the claim includes interest or other charges in addition to the principal amount of the claim. Attach a statement that itemizes interest or charges.

2. Basis for Claim: Money Loaned
(See instruction #2)

3. Last four digits of any number by which creditor identifies debtor: **3a. Debtor may have scheduled account as:**   **3b. Uniform Claim Identifier (optional):**

(See instruction #3a)   (See instruction #3b)

4. Secured Claim (See instruction #4)
Check the appropriate box if the claim is secured by a lien on property or a right of setoff, attach required redacted documents, and provide the requested information.

Nature of property or right of setoff: ☑Real Estate ☐Motor Vehicle ☐Other
Describe: 2429-31 Bolton Road, Fulton County, Georgia

Value of Property: $_____

Annual Interest Rate_____% ☐Fixed or ☐Variable
(when case was filed)

Amount of arrearage and other charges, as of the time case was filed, included in secured claim, if any:

$_____

Basis for perfection: Recorded Security Deed

Amount of Secured Claim: $ 535,000.00

Amount Unsecured: $ 0.00

5. Amount of Claim Entitled to Priority under 11 U.S.C. § 507 (a). If any part of the claim falls into one of the following categories, check the box specifying the priority and state the amount.

☐ Domestic support obligations under 11 U.S.C. § 507 (a)(1)(A) or (a)(1)(B).

☐ Wages, salaries, or commissions (up to $12,475*) earned within 180 days before the case was filed or the debtor's business ceased, whichever is earlier – 11 U.S.C. § 507 (a)(4).

☐ Contributions to an employee benefit plan – 11 U.S.C. § 507 (a)(5).

☐ Up to $2,775* of deposits toward purchase, lease, or rental of property or services for personal, family, or household use – 11 U.S.C. § 507 (a)(7).

☐ Taxes or penalties owed to governmental units – 11 U.S.C. § 507 (a)(8).

☐ Other – Specify applicable paragraph of 11 U.S.C. § 507 (a)(__).

Amount entitled to priority:
$_____

*Amounts are subject to adjustment on 4/01/16 and every 3 years thereafter with respect to cases commenced on or after the date of adjustment.

6. Credits. The amount of all payments on this claim has been credited for the purpose of making this proof of claim. (See instruction #6)

- The top of the page requires basic information about the case name, name and address of the creditor, and other contact information.
- Section 3 requires the creditor to state the basis of the claim. This is usually "money loaned" or "auto loan" or "real estate mortgage." Something along those lines.
- Section 4 requires the creditor to state whether the claim is secured, and if so, to describe the collateral, provide the loan amount, the balance due (the secured claim), the interest rate, and any arrearage owed. If there is no security, just the amounts are necessary.

B10 (Official Form 10) (04/13)   2

7. Documents: Attached are redacted copies of any documents that support the claim, such as promissory notes, purchase orders, invoices, itemized statements of running accounts, contracts, judgments, mortgages, security agreements, or, in the case of a claim based on an open-end or revolving consumer credit agreement, a statement providing the information required by FRBP 3001(c)(3)(A). If the claim is secured, box 4 has been completed, and redacted copies of documents providing evidence of perfection of a security interest are attached. If the claim is secured by the debtor's principal residence, the Mortgage Proof of Claim Attachment is being filed with this claim. (See instruction #7, and the definition of "redacted".)

DO NOT SEND ORIGINAL DOCUMENTS. ATTACHED DOCUMENTS MAY BE DESTROYED AFTER SCANNING.

If the documents are not available, please explain: Based on settlement agreement with Trustee [Doc. 73 and 74]

8. Signature: (See instruction #8.)

Check the appropriate box.

☐ I am the creditor.   ☑ I am the creditor's authorized agent.   ☐ I am the trustee, or the debtor,   ☐ I am a guarantor, surety, indorser, or other codebtor.
                                                         or their authorized agent.   (See Bankruptcy Rule 3005.)
                                                         (See Bankruptcy Rule 3004.)

I declare under penalty of perjury that the information provided in this claim is true and correct to the best of my knowledge, information, and reasonable belief.

Print Name: Scott B. Kuperberg, Esq.
Title: Counsel for Creditor
Company: Busch, Slipakoff & Schuh, LLP
Address and telephone number (if different from notice address above):   (Signature)   4/8/2013
                                                                                                         (Date)

Telephone number: email:
Penalty for presenting fraudulent claim: Fine of up to $500,000 or imprisonment for up to 5 years, or both. 18 U.S.C. §§ 152 and 3571.

INSTRUCTIONS FOR PROOF OF CLAIM FORM
The instructions and definitions below are general explanations of the law. In certain circumstances, such as bankruptcy cases not filed voluntarily by the debtor, exceptions to these general rules may apply.
Items to be completed in Proof of Claim form

Court, Name of Debtor, and Case Number:
Fill in the federal judicial district in which the bankruptcy case was filed (for example, Central District of California), the debtor's full name, and the case number. If the creditor received a notice of the case from the bankruptcy court, all of this information is at the top of the notice.

Creditor's Name and Address:
Fill in the name of the person or entity asserting a claim and the name and address of the person who should receive notices issued during the bankruptcy case. A separate space is provided for the payment address if it differs from the notice address. The creditor has a continuing obligation to keep the court informed of its current address. See Federal Rule of Bankruptcy Procedure (FRBP) 2002(g).

1. Amount of Claim as of Date Case Filed:
State the total amount owed to the creditor on the date of the bankruptcy filing. Follow the instructions concerning whether to complete items 4 and 5. Check the box if interest or other charges are included in the claim.

2. Basis for Claim:
State the type of debt or how it was incurred. Examples include goods sold, money loaned, services performed, personal injury/wrongful death, car loan, mortgage note, and credit card. If the claim is based on delivering health care goods or services, limit the disclosure of the goods or services so as to avoid embarrassment or the disclosure of confidential health care information. You may be required to provide additional disclosure if an interested party objects to the claim.

3. Last Four Digits of Any Number by Which Creditor Identifies Debtor:
State only the last four digits of the debtor's account or other number used by the creditor to identify the debtor.

3a. Debtor May Have Scheduled Account As:
Report a change in the creditor's name, a transferred claim, or any other information that clarifies a difference between this proof of claim and the claim as scheduled by the debtor.

3b. Uniform Claim Identifier:
If you use a uniform claim identifier, you may report it here. A uniform claim identifier is an optional 24-character identifier that certain large creditors use to facilitate electronic payment in chapter 13 cases.

4. Secured Claim:
Check whether the claim is fully or partially secured. Skip this section if the

claim is entirely unsecured. (See Definitions.) If the claim is secured, check the box for the nature and value of property that secures the claim, attach copies of lien documentation, and state, as of the date of the bankruptcy filing, the annual interest rate (and whether it is fixed or variable), and the amount past due on the claim.

5. Amount of Claim Entitled to Priority Under 11 U.S.C. § 507 (a).
If any portion of the claim falls into any category shown, check the appropriate box(es) and state the amount entitled to priority. (See Definitions.) A claim may be partly priority and partly non-priority. For example, in some of the categories, the law limits the amount entitled to priority.

6. Credits:
An authorized signature on this proof of claim serves as an acknowledgment that when calculating the amount of the claim, the creditor gave the debtor credit for any payments received toward the debt.

7. Documents:
Attach redacted copies of any documents that show the debt exists and a lien secures the debt. You must also attach copies of documents that evidence perfection of any security interest and documents required by FRBP 3001(c) for claims based on an open-end or revolving consumer credit agreement or secured by a security interest in the debtor's principal residence. You may also attach a summary in addition to the documents themselves. FRBP 3001(c) and (d). If the claim is based on delivering health care goods or services, limit disclosing confidential health care information. Do not send original documents, as attachments may be destroyed after scanning.

8. Date and Signature:
The individual completing this proof of claim must sign and date it. FRBP 9011. If the claim is filed electronically, FRBP 5005(a)(2) authorizes courts to establish local rules specifying what constitutes a signature. If you sign this form, you declare under penalty of perjury that the information provided is true and correct to the best of your knowledge, information, and reasonable belief. Your signature is also a certification that the claim meets the requirements of FRBP 9011(b). Whether the claim is filed electronically or in person, if your name is on the signature line, you are responsible for the declaration. Print the name and title, if any, of the creditor or other person authorized to file this claim. State the filer's address and telephone number if it differs from the address given on the top of the form for purposes of receiving notices. If the claim is filed by an authorized agent, provide both the name of the individual filing the claim and the name of the agent. If the authorized agent is a servicer, identify the corporate servicer as the company. Criminal penalties apply for making a false statement on a proof of claim.

- If the claim is secured, the creditor is required to attach a copy of the security agreement, or other document that shows that the claim is secured. This is usually the mortgage or security deed, car lien, or UCC-1 statement. If you do not have a copy of the document, you have to explain on this page why there is no security document.

CHAPTER VII

Case Studies and Best Practices for Your Industry

General Considerations for Written Agreements with Customers

Most businesses that work with consumers will have a written agreement for anything other than an outright cash sale on the spot. Even then, you'll have a receipt. If you are going to have any sort of relationship with a consumer beyond a point-of-sale transaction, make sure there are documents to memorialize the transaction. A handshake is worthless in bankruptcy court. Get everything in writing.

Make sure that your loan agreements contain language that void the agreement due to insolvency giving the creditor the right to seize the collateral pursuant to state law. Make sure that your documents are signed and witnessed properly as required by your state law. If you're taking a security interest, make sure your security instrument is recorded properly and has the correct notary and witness seals. There have been many cases where secured status was denied for an improperly recorded or signed document.

Venders and Suppliers

Often in your business, you are shipping products on credit. At the time that you begin a relationship with a client where you'll be shipping on credit (direct credit, not through a finance company that pays you up front), file a UCC-1 statement on all goods sold and on all inventory. This will give you secured creditor status in the event your customer goes bankrupt. Also make sure your finance agreements declare a default when the buyer becomes insolvent. This will void the contract and make the entire debt due.

Keep extremely accurate books and records. Record all payments and keep copies of all invoices and payment demands. Make sure your accounting system can accurately show a third party how payments are applied to principle, interest, and late fees. The single biggest problem creditors have in bankruptcy court is explaining to a judge how they arrived at their figure for the debt owed. It happens in every industry.

Consumer Lenders

Consumer lenders would do well to read the aforesaid advice, specifically related to contracts and keeping accurate financial records. If you're a purchase money lender, for example, selling a TV on store credit, you are entitled to file a UCC-1 statement to secure your rights to seize the TV. Now, one has to do the math to see if the goods you're selling are worth the great effort to become a secured creditor in the event of a consumer bankruptcy. Insurance is available for businesses to protect their accounts receivable.

If your line of business is unsecured consumer lending, not purchase money, be sure to closely follow the rules of the automatic stay. As we said previously, once a bankruptcy case is filed, unsecured creditors have little recourse or hope of recovering money. Monitor a Chapter 13 case closely and, perhaps, do what you can to get it dismissed. This will restore the debt.

Landlords and Tenants

Landlords, whether commercial or residential, are subject to the automatic bankruptcy stay just like all other creditors. How you treat a debtor in bankruptcy depends on your goals. If the debtor intends, and is able to, continue occupying the property and paying rent, a landlord can enter into an agreement with the debtor to continue paying rent during the term of the bankruptcy, and allowing the debtor's lease to survive the bankruptcy.

However, if the debtor is unable to pay, the landlord must get relief from the automatic stay to proceed with eviction. If the bankruptcy case is pending during the eviction, the landlord is not permitted to sue for unpaid rent or damages. These claims must be made part of the bankruptcy case.

Mortgage Lenders

Mortgage lenders generally require the assistance of an attorney. As a secured creditor, with the collateral being real property, a mortgage lender can ask the bankruptcy court to lift the automatic stay to proceed with state law foreclosure. However, in Chapter 13, if the lender is receiving "adequate protection," meaning payments sufficient to secure the value of the collateral (equivalent to the correct mortgage payment), the lender cannot seek foreclosure.

Mortgage lenders have to confirm that the subject property is insured and that taxes have been paid. The mortgage lender will want to do their own independent appraisal of the property to confirm the value, relative to the debt owed.

Because of the explosion of foreclosures, courts have begun to scrutinize mortgage lenders more carefully. Make sure that you have all deeds and security instruments signed and witnessed properly as required by your state law. Make sure everything is recorded with the appropriate authority. Improperly signed or recorded documents may void a lender's security interest.

The single biggest hurdle mortgage lenders face in bankruptcy court is numbers. Mortgage lenders are notoriously bad at keeping track of payments and applying those payments properly to calculate outstanding debt or arrearage. I've heard many judges say from the bench, on the record, that they don't trust any numbers provided by a mortgage lender, because they have been allowed to fudge the math for so many decades.

It is imperative that you keep accurate records of all payments and a running total of the payment application and balance due. You must be able to explain to the court how each number was calculated, and show the method of calculation based on the loan contract. This is an onerous burden on mortgage lenders today. But according to numerous bankruptcy judges I've spoken to over the years, it is a consequence of shoddy work that the industry has endured for the last 30 years.

Community Associations

Countless community and homeowners associations exist throughout the United States. They come in every form from subdivisions to condominiums. Homeowner bankruptcy is a huge problem for homeowners associations who cannot collect membership dues from insolvent homeowners.

In most cases, the community association will be considered a secured creditor. Many state statutes provide for automatic (statutory) liens on real property for unpaid membership dues. Even so, it is still best to file a claim or notice of lien in the county real estate records if an arrearage builds up. This will save time and money explaining to an uninitiated bankruptcy judge the process of the statutory lien.

In a Chapter 7 case, most homeowners will be surrendering their real property to the mortgage lender. In this case, the Association is essentially out of luck and will likely never be able to collect the unpaid assessments. This can be especially frustrating since lenders take time to foreclose upon, and take title to, the real property. During that gap period, the association can generally not demand collection, nor attempt to collect after the bankruptcy is over. Some states have proposed statutes under debate to deal with this gap period.

In a Chapter 13 case where the debtor intends to keep their real property, the debtor is liable to pay assessments as they come due during the course of the bankruptcy case, as well as the arrearage. The arrearage will be accounted for in the Chapter 13 Plan. The debtor must show in his Schedules that he can afford to continue to pay assessments. Otherwise the association can ask the bankruptcy court to dismiss the case based on an unfeasible Plan.

If an association is not getting paid, there are precious few options. An association could theoretically ask the court to lift the automatic stay and allow the association to foreclose its lien, if permitted by state law. However, in most cases, the association's lien is either inferior to the mortgage lender, disallowing the foreclosure, or the foreclosed property would still have the mortgage lender's lien on title, limiting the sale possibilities.

It is important for community associations to work with attorneys expert in the field of association law. Each state has its own unique legal regime. The best practice for homeowners associations is to keep up with collection and lien filing, and keep meticulous records of billing and payment.

Case Study—"When the Liquor Distributor Went Bankrupt"

The most unique case I ever dealt with involved liquor. I represented a liquor importing company that was a creditor in a bankruptcy case. The debtor was a liquor distributorship. The importer gave the distributor liquor, based on orders, to sell on consignment. Then the distributor sells the liquor to stores and pays the importer back from the profits. One would think this should be a thriving business. But when this distributor went bankrupt, he owed my client in excess of $90,000.00. And all of the liquor that was consigned with the distributor was still in the warehouse.

The first question the trustee asked when we all gathered together was, "How in the world does a liquor distributorship go out of business?!" We were all baffled. The trustee brought in a liquor law expert to assist with licensing and valuation. The distributor was indebted to his landlord for several hundred thousand dollars. The entire balance of the unpaid lease came due. Very quickly, the landlord became the top priority creditor.

My client demanded that we simply seize the liquor. However, my client broke the cardinal rule of doing business: he did not have anything in writing. All we had to go by was a shipping report and my client's word of the value. There were no consignment agreements, no contracts, no liens, no notes. The trustee accepted our claim, but we did not have enough evidence to get relief from stay to seize the liquor. Nor could we claim priority status as a secured creditor. The trustee proposed to sell the liquor, somehow, to pay off the creditors.

Aside from our inability to get paid or get the inventory returned, my client insisted that under state liquor law, a trustee could not sell liquor without a license. Case law and the judge said otherwise. The trustee, apparently, stepped into the shoes of the distributor, licensed and all, when the bankruptcy case was filed. My client was livid.

In the end, the liquor was sold for 1/10th its value, and my client got nothing. No cash, no returned inventory. The case took over two years to resolve. But the lesson was learned: always get your agreements in writing. My client's willingness to do big business on a handshake cost him tens of thousands of dollars.

CHAPTER VIII

Post-Bankruptcy—The Relationship Continues?

Effect of Bankruptcy Dismissal

At whatever stage it occurs, a bankruptcy dismissal puts the parties back as they were. The automatic stay is immediately lifted, meaning collection action can be taken again. All debts that were due before are due again, less any payments made.

In the event of a dismissal, your relationship with the debtor continues as it was before. You are entitled to add on interest and late fees that accrued during the bankruptcy. You may reinstitute or continue any lawsuits that were pending against the debtor.

There are rare cases when a bankruptcy case is dismissed and then reopened. There are grounds where a judge will allow a case to be reopened, such as illness, mistake, in the interest of justice. It is important to debtors that a case be reopened rather than refiled. There are adverse consequences to filing multiple bankruptcy cases. Fortunately for the creditor, any action taken during the time the case was dismissed is valid, and not a violation of the automatic stay. So once a case is dismissed, it is best to continue your collection action immediately.

Multiple dismissals within a given period of time may disallow the debtor from filing again, or if he does file, the debtor may not receive protection under the automatic stay. Multiple filings in a short time following multiple dismissals give rise to a presumption of fraud (11 U.S.C. 362(c)(3)).

Bankruptcy Discharge

A bankruptcy discharge order means that all debts owed that did not survive the bankruptcy are now uncollectable. In Chapter 7, this means all debts that were not subject to a reaffirmation agreement. If you do not have a reaffirmation agreement, and your lien on any secured property survived the bankruptcy, you may now proceed with foreclosure. But the debt itself is uncollectable. If you did have a reaffirmation agreement, your relationship with the debtor continues under the terms of the reaffirmation agreement. In Chapter 13, this means all debts owed on abandoned collateral, and all debts on unsecured claims are now uncollectable. Similar to Chapter 7, if there is surviving collateral with a surviving lien, the creditor may proceed with foreclosure.

A strong note of caution: It is a violation of bankruptcy law to attempt to collect a debt that has been discharged in bankruptcy. Attempted collection of a discharged debt is as severe a violation as trying to collect a debt in violation of the automatic stay.

Make sure to consult with your attorney after the bankruptcy case has been concluded about how you may proceed with the collection of unpaid debts and recovering collateral.

CHAPTER IX

In Case You Were Wondering...

There are several other types of bankruptcy. You will hear about one or more of these commonly in the media. While they are generally not related to consumer bankruptcy, it seems appropriate to at least give them a mention.

Chapter 9—Municipality Bankruptcy

The federal government is allowed by law to operate in a deficit. States, cities, and towns are generally not allowed this same privilege. It happens from time to time that a city goes bankrupt. In other words, the city is unable to meet its legally obligated payments. These payments can include benefits to workers and citizens, payments on outstanding debt like municipal bonds, and operating expenses.

A famous recent example is the bankruptcy of the City of Detroit. At the time of publication, the case is ongoing. In reaching agreements with creditors, the City of Detroit has agreed to drastic cutbacks in employee salaries, operating budgets, and public entitlements. The city is also selling off assets like priceless works of art.

This form of bankruptcy is very rare, but it has a severe impact on the region of the bankrupt municipality.

Chapter 11—Corporate Reorganization and Wealthy Consumers

There are two types of Chapter 11 bankruptcy. The most well known is corporate reorganization or unwinding. Reorganization was done by General Motors in 2008 to 2009. Whereas Pan Am, a number of years back, used bankruptcy to shut down. This is like Chapter 13 for corporate entities. There is even a Chapter 11 Plan of Reorganization.

The second type of Chapter 11 is for individuals who meet a certain wealth threshold. Their bankruptcies are too complicated for the Chapter 7 or Chapter 13 system with numerous creditors and more experts needed to value and sell off assets. If you encounter a Chapter 11 consumer bankruptcy, go immediately to an expert attorney. Do not even consider attempting to navigate this extremely complex form of bankruptcy on your own, without an attorney's guidance.

Chapter 12—Family Farmers and Fishermen

This author has encountered two Chapter 12 bankruptcies in his career. Both were related to family farms. Very few judges have experience with this chapter of the bankruptcy code, and often experts are called in to assist. Bankruptcy law gives special consideration to consumers whose primary line of work is farming or fishing. Assets and debts of farmers and fisherman do not fall neatly into the categories of Chapter 7 and Chapter 13 bankruptcies. Farmers typically operate on a different system of financing from banks than ordinary consumers. Also, the valuation of crops is a specialized matter. Operationally, a Chapter 12 bankruptcy is similar to Chapter 13. Again, if you run into this type of bankruptcy, proceed immediately to a qualified lawyer to assist.

Chapter 15—International Bankruptcy

This is a special form of bankruptcy for multinational corporations. Again, because of the unique structure of financing multinational companies, and marshalling and disposing of assets in multiple countries, experts and a special system of bankruptcy law are called into play.

Conclusion

If you receive a bankruptcy notice from one of your customers, do not despair. Part of doing business is dealing with customers who may never pay. The bankruptcy code and process give business creditors some chance and hope of recovering their unpaid debts. A wise man once said, this just is business, not personal. Keep your head, make wise decisions, keep great records, and you will navigate this maze of bankruptcy successfully.

References

11 U.S.C. § 1300 et seq.

11 U.S.C. § 1301

11 U.S.C. § 300 et seq.

11 U.S.C. § 341

11 U.S.C. § 362

11 U.S.C. § 500 et seq.

11 U.S.C. § 521

11 U.S.C. § 522

11 U.S.C. § 541

11 U.S.C. § 544

11 U.S.C. § 700 et seq.

Hubbard v. Fleet Mortgage, 810 F.2d 778 (8th Cir. 1987)

Index

OTHER TITLES IN OUR BUSINESS LAW COLLECTION

John Wood, Econautics Sustainability Institute, Editor

- *Preventing Litigation: An Early Warning System to Get Big Value out of Big Data* by Nelson E. Brestoff and William H. Inmon
- *Light on Peacemaking: A Guide to Appropriate Dispute Resolution and Mediating Family Conflict* by Thomas DiGrazia

Business Expert Press has over 30 collection in business subjects such as finance, marketing strategy, sustainability, public relations, economics, accounting, corporate communications, and many others. For more information about all our collections, please visit www.businessexpertpress.com/collections.

Business Expert Press is actively seeking collection editors as well as authors. For more information about becoming an BEP author or collection editor, please visit http://www.businessexpertpress.com/author

Announcing the Business Expert Press Digital Library

Concise e-books business students need for classroom and research

This book can also be purchased in an e-book collection by your library as

- a one-time purchase,
- that is owned forever,
- allows for simultaneous readers,
- has no restrictions on printing, and
- can be downloaded as PDFs from within the library community.

Our digital library collections are a great solution to beat the rising cost of textbooks. E-books can be loaded into their course management systems or onto students' e-book readers.
The **Business Expert Press** digital libraries are very affordable, with no obligation to buy in future years. For more information, please visit **www.businessexpertpress.com/librarians**. To set up a trial in the United States, please email **sales@businessexpertpress.com**.

CPSIA information can be obtained
at www.ICGtesting.com
Printed in the USA
LVOW13s0059231216

518487LV00013B/133/P

9 781631 572487